Responding to God's Call

Responding to God's Call

Christian formation today

Jeremy Worthen

CANTERBURY
PRESS
Norwich

© Jeremy Worthen 2012

First published in 2012 by the Canterbury Press Norwich
Editorial office
3rd Floor, Invicta House,
108–114 Golden Lane,
London EC1Y 0TG

Canterbury Press is an imprint of Hymns Ancient & Modern Ltd
(a registered charity)
13A Hellesdon Park Road, Norwich,
Norfolk, NR6 5DR, UK

www.canterburypress.co.uk

Scriptural quotations are taken from The Holy Bible Containing
the Old and New Revised Standard Version, 1995, Oxford University Press,
unless otherwise indicated.

British Library Cataloguing in Publication data

A catalogue record for this book is available from the British Library

978 1 84825 212 7

Typeset by Manila Typesetting
Printed and bound in Great Britain by
CPI Group, Croydon

Contents

Foreword		ix
Preface		xi
Acknowledgements		xix

Part 1 How Life Shapes Us   **1**

1 Freedom   **5**

Modern developments: from dependence
to autonomy   6

Contemporary issues: expressive
individualism   9

Crosscurrents in formation: vocation
and selfhood   13

2 Knowledge   **17**

Modern developments: dare to know   18

Contemporary issues: the limits
of knowledge   20

Crosscurrents in formation: tradition
and rationality   23

3 Love   **28**

Modern developments: romance and
the novel   29

Contemporary issues: unstable
relationships   32

Crosscurrents in formation: love and duty   35

CONTENTS

Part 2 Understanding Christian Vocation   **39**

    4   **Called in Creation**   **43**
        Called into relation with the earth   44
        Called into relation with one another   47
        Called into relation with God   50
        Formation as human creatures   53

    5   **Called through Christ**   **58**
        Jesus the bearer of God's call   59
        Jesus the hearer of God's call   64
        God the only Son   69
        The image of the invisible God   72

    6   **Responding as the Church**   **77**
        The purpose of God's call   77
        Shared response: the sacraments of
          the Church   80
        Distinctive vocations: vocations of
          daily life   86
        Distinctive vocations: vocations of
          Christian ministry   91

Part 3 Making Space for Christian Formation   **99**

    7   **Remembering**   **105**
        Forming our memory   105
        Liturgical formation   111
        Fractured memory   117
        Spiritual formation: meditation   121

    8   **Understanding**   **126**
        Forming the understanding   126
        Theological formation   130
        Partial understanding   136
        Spiritual formation: contemplation   142

CONTENTS

9   Willing   **148**
   Forming the will   148
   Moral formation   152
   Divided will   158
   Spiritual formation: election   164

Afterword   169
Further Reading   173
Index   175

Foreword

'I wanted to change the world,' goes the one liner, 'but I couldn't get a baby sitter.' Some processes are rather more complex than a quick-fix culture wants to admit. One such process is what we call Christian formation.

Contrary to what many think, this is not an esoteric experience for a few people strangely called to be ordained, but rather it's the common life of the people of God, shaped with one degree of intentionality or another into Christian discipleship. It happens through the normal pressures and experiences of life, through the absorption of theological understanding from a variety of formal and less formal sources, and through the experience of worship and fellowship in the church. We are all being shaped and formed in ways that might both encourage and alarm us if we knew what was really happening.

Within the formational experience that is common to the people of God there often arises the possibility of a distinct vocation which requires specific elements of formational experience. One of these vocations is to ordained ministry. This is a calling of wonderful and terrifying potential which requires of the candidate an orientation towards God, society and individual people that will stretch and pinch, elate and deflate, inspire and conspire in varying measures.

What we need in this crucible of Christian formation is someone who can map the territory and identify the processes. We need someone who is alert to the layers of meaning in the word 'formation' and can give some theological ballast to the process. We need an erudite Christian mind and an elegant writer.

Fortunately, we have such a person. Jeremy Worthen is one of the most perceptive participant observers in the field of theological education. Here he offers the wisdom of many years of direct involvement and careful reflection on what's really going on in Christian formation. He starts wide and then narrows the focus, but always he offers the dimension of depth. Here are profoundly helpful avenues of understanding for all Christians who want to reflect on what is going on as we grow up into Christ.

As a result, we may not change the world, but we might change that bit of the world in which we are set. With or without a baby-sitter.

+John Pritchard

Preface

For many of the people whom I hope might read this book, Christian formation will not be a familiar phrase and may sound like a subject for specialists only. On the other hand, for clergy, faculty and Church officers who work in areas to do with adult education and training for ministry, whom I also hope might read it, 'formation' has become something of a jargon term in the course of the past twenty years. While in such circles it is generally agreed that it is a good thing, and perhaps even a very important thing, it is not necessarily all that clear what sort of thing it actually is. So when I started to tell people that I was writing a book on Christian formation, I tended to get one of two responses. Colleagues and clergy were for the most part interested in and even enthusiastic about what they thought I was doing – but I sometimes wondered if we might be talking at cross-purposes. On the other hand, people from the congregation of my local church looked blank or just came straight back at me by asking: 'What's that?'

Before I try to give an answer to that question, it might be helpful to sketch something of the background to my own interest in this area. Back in 1999, I was paying my first visit as a relatively new staff member at the South East Institute for Theological Education (usually abbreviated as SEITE) to Bovendonk, a Roman Catholic seminary in the Netherlands with which we have a link. In the car from the railway station back to the seminary, the Rector asked me how I was finding my new role in formation. I can remember being somewhat taken aback by his question. This was not how I thought about what I was doing, and while I had heard the word used occasionally, I was not all that sure what it actually meant. Still, over time I began to appreciate his understanding of formation and how it related both to official documents of the Roman Catholic Church and the work of the Institute of Psychology of the Gregorian University, where he had completed advanced studies.[i]

SEITE was different from Bovendonk in all kinds of ways: an ecumenical organization, predominantly Anglican, which taught theology to lay people as well as those preparing for ordained ministry. Although there were many things I missed from working as an Anglican priest in a parish, it was becoming clear that there was both tremendous privilege and responsibility in being with people who were passing through seasons of profound change. Not that this was true of all students all of the time, but it was true of many of the students for some of the time. The catalyst could be one or more from a number of factors: encountering perspectives from academic theology for the first time; praying with people from different traditions of faith; beginning to inhabit ministerial roles; facing the reality of what the Church expects of ordained ministers; opening up new friendships where high levels of trust could be reached in a very short time; and what one might refer to as the changes and chances of this mortal life. All of that weaving together made for a particular kind of climate, which seemed to nurture, though not compel, a particular kind of growing. This growing was spiritual, personal, intellectual, ministerial – and somehow about how all of these came together. So it was at SEITE, and so it was too at Bovendonk. But they had a word for this process of

---

i Matt Ham, ed., 2011, *Late Have I Loved You: Part-time Priestly Formation for Adults: Psycho-spiritual Aspects*, ET, Raleigh, North Carolina: Lulu Press, pp. 52–164.

being shaped as whole persons for specific vocations in the life of the Church: formation.

Over the next few years, I increasingly found this same word becoming part of the mainstream discourse for Anglicans and Protestants around education and training for ministry – at least at the institutional centre, where it has figured in the title of major reports, departments and official bodies in the UK churches. Meaning in this context, however, lacking the anchorage in official teaching that it has in Roman Catholic circles, can vary quite significantly.[ii] It is sometimes used in a comparable way to describe the whole process of structured preparation for ministry, encompassing theological education, practical training and spiritual and personal growth, all in the context of a community life that has worship at its heart. Yet it can also be treated as roughly equivalent to the personal and spiritual growth needed for public ministry, and therefore as something additional to and indeed separable from theological education and practical training. (It still happens that occasionally people tell me a candidate for ordained ministry has done all the necessary study and practised all the relevant skills, so now 'just' needs formation.) In some ways this reflects the broader usage of the term in secular literature on professional development. Moreover, even when formation is used in the first, holistic sense, common meaning requires some kind of agreement about the purpose of this integrated process and its characteristic opportunities and challenges. Yet my experience has been that such agreement is not at all easy to establish, even within a single institution, let alone within or even between denominations.

This book, then, originates from my conviction that formation does indeed need to be a central concept for Christian

---

ii Charles R. Foster, Lisa Dahill, Lawrence A. Golemon and Barbara Wang Tolentino, 2006, *Educating Clergy: Teaching Practices and Pastoral Imagination*, San Francisco: Jossey-Bass; Ian Bunting, 2009, 'Formation and Validity', *Journal of Adult Theological Education*, 6.1, pp. 8–30.

education and training today across a whole range of contexts (not limited to ordained ministry), and from my concern that it is too often used as a concept without any clear content. While as an Anglican working in an ecumenical context I do not expect – nor do I seek – the same kind of precision that can be found in Roman Catholic documents, I do need to be able to give some account of what I mean by it.[iii] Indeed, if I want those I am teaching to understand themselves as being 'in formation', then I owe them some kind of explanation that they can consider, reflect on and respond to, even if it is to tell me that they do not agree with it or find it irrelevant to their experience.

What, then, is Christian formation? As I talk about it here, Christian formation refers to the ways in which Christians are shaped in and for vocation, where vocation names the process of responding to God's call. There is a shared call for all Christians, and a shared vocation that follows from this: the call to follow Christ and be conformed to his image as the Son of God. There is a unique call for each Christian and a unique vocation that follows from this: the journey of discipleship is never identical for two or more people and unfolds along the pathways of each unrepeatable life. Finally, there are what we might call distinctive calls and distinctive vocations that follow from them: most Christians would agree on ordained ministry (though not necessarily on how to describe it) as one of these, some would add the religious life, and others might want to extend this category to marriage and types of work. Yet there is also only one call and one vocation: our unique and distinctive vocations are not additional vocations to the shared vocation of following Jesus, but different ways in which together we live our single, common vocation.

---

iii For an exploration of 'common denominators' in Anglican ministerial formation, see Martyn Percy, 2010, *Shaping the Church: The Promise of Implicit Theology*, Farnham: Ashgate, pp. 131–42.

If that is right, then all Christians are in formation, as all Christians are being shaped in and for their vocation in Christ. Of course, there will be times when we are particularly conscious of this shaping: for instance, as we are preparing to take a new step or assume a new responsibility (when we may be acutely aware of how far we are from what we are called to be). While ordained ministry is the obvious example here, it is also not necessarily the most helpful place to start; indeed, the way that ordination has tended to monopolize the language of vocation and formation in Western Christianity has arguably been seriously detrimental for Christian discipleship. It might be better to see preparation for baptism as the paradigm for Christian formation: getting ready to die with Christ so that we might rise with Christ and live as part of his body in communion with the Triune God.[iv] Just as we need to keep growing into the fullness of our baptismal calling through the whole of our Christian lives, so we need to let the process of Christian formation associated with that baptism extend to everything that we do after it and reach into the inmost depths of our being. Moreover, beginning with baptism might also help us to understand that formation and mission are inseparable, rather than being tempted to view them as competing priorities: formation for baptism is formation for witness. If there is no evidence of those baptized into Christ being formed in the likeness of Christ, why on earth should anyone believe the good news that the Lord is risen?

As I hope is already apparent, I am passionately concerned about the formation of ordained ministers and delighted that this book is being published by Canterbury Press alongside widely respected works on *Being a Priest Today* and *Being a*

---

iv Aidan Kavanagh, 1978, *The Shape of Baptism: The Rite of Christian Initiation*, New York: Pueblo, pp. 154–63.

*Deacon Today.*ᵛ I pray that it will be of some value to people at all
stages of the journey who want to explore what it might mean
to be shaped by a calling to specific ministry. Yet I am also con-
vinced that ministerial formation can only be understood from
the perspective of Christian formation for the whole Church.
Indeed, as late modernity corrodes the remaining traces of
Christendom, which might itself be defined by the embedding
of Christian formation in dominant social practices, attention
to Christian formation becomes ever more imperative for all
Christian communities and indeed all committed disciples.
Hence this is not just a book for clergy and ministry students,
as will I trust become apparent as you read on.

The three parts of the book, each containing three chapters,
follow from the understanding of Christian formation outlined
here. We are shaped in and for vocation, but we are clearly
shaped by many other things as well. What are some of the
characteristic ways in which we are formed by our society and
culture at the start of the twenty-first century, and how might
they relate to Christian formation? That is the question at the
heart of Part 1. In order to understand Christian formation at
any depth on this basis, however, we need to explore the meaning of Christian vocation: how does God call us, and what does
this have to do with the great themes of Christian teaching such
as creation, incarnation, salvation, Church and mission? Part
2 seeks to outline some answers. Finally, while formation is
God's work, it also asks for our attention, energy and effort in
making space for the activity of the Spirit, who alone can form
us into the likeness of Christ. Part 3 reflects on how we can
draw on some of the many riches of Christian tradition in the

v Rosalind Brown, 2005, *Being a Deacon Today: Exploring a Distinctive Ministry in the Church and in the World*, Norwich: Canterbury Press; Christopher Cocksworth and Rosalind Brown, 2006, *Being a Priest Today: Exploring Priestly Identity*, 2nd edn, Norwich: Canterbury Press.

contemporary context to guide us in being open to formation ourselves and in supporting the formation of others.

My hope is that these three parts make a coherent whole and that some readers at least will benefit by reading through its chapters in sequence. As someone who has worked with part-time students for many years, however, I am also aware that not everyone who picks up this book will have the time or the inclination to read it cover to cover. Moreover, although there are good reasons for presenting the material in Part 1 as vital background, it is likely to be hard going for some and does not address so directly as Part 2 the personal and spiritual concerns that might move some people to open a book on Christian formation, nor so clearly as Part 3 issues about the life of Christian communities that might have prompted others. It should be possible to use the introductions at the start of each Part to locate the material that is of most interest to you within the approach of the book as a whole and perhaps to begin there, moving out into other sections as and when you need to. A brief review of key points also appears at the end of each chapter.

Acknowledgements

I owe many debts to many people for their help, knowingly or unknowingly given, with the book that follows. It can seem that I have had some kind of conversation about it with just about everyone I have met over the past couple of years, as well as giving related talks to various groups including the College of Canons at Chichester Cathedral and the Rochester Theological Society. I am deeply grateful to the Council of SEITE for enabling me to take sabbatical leave from all other responsibilities to focus (finally) on this task at the start of 2012. As part of that, in January I spent the most wonderful month at Vaughan Park Anglican Retreat Centre just outside Auckland in New Zealand as a writer in residence; such coherence as is found here owes much to Vaughan Park's unique spaces, communal, spiritual and geographical. Conversation over meals with other guests fed my thinking; Christine Sorenson was particularly helpful. The Director of Vaughan Park, John Fairbrother, listened patiently through the highs and lows of the writing process and sustained it with his interest in the subject and his critical engagement with my thinking. My thanks go to John and Margaret and to the whole staff team at Vaughan Park for their welcome, and to its Board for making my time there possible. Once I was back in England, John Fairbrother, Peter Ingrams, Sheridan James, Tim Ling, Martyn Percy and Hannah Worthen provided helpful comments on initial versions of the text. They illuminated some of its shortcomings and helped me to address them, though I know that many remain. Without the support and encouragement of Lizzie, my wife, none of this would have been possible.

It also needs to be acknowledged, however, that this book has grown first and foremost out of my work at SEITE over close to fifteen years. It has been nurtured through innumerable exchanges with colleagues and students over that period. Much of the material that follows first began to emerge through teaching the course on 'Persons in Relation and Formation' and was then refined and expanded through the creative interaction arising from it. Above all, however, it is only because students at SEITE have been prepared to share something of their joys and struggles, indeed something of themselves, with me as a member of staff that I have been able to reflect with any real depth on what formation in and for vocation might actually be like. I am deeply grateful to them all.

PART 1

How Life Shapes Us

Christian formation does not happen to people who are not being formed in any other way. Life is always forming us and shaping us. We are formed by our upbringing, by our education, by our work. We are formed by the cultures in which we participate – the TV we watch, the books we read, the way we use technology. We are formed by the societies in which we live, with their complex legal, political and economic systems. All of these activities communicate, more or less explicitly, narratives of human fulfilment: they imply stories about what is desirable, what brings happiness, what will enable us to become who we are, as well as what will be punished or end in disaster – and they also inevitably screen out other stories from our attention. We do not need to be able to articulate those narratives in order to be powerfully influenced by them: we just have to participate in the activities that communicate and affirm them. What forms us is not primarily a matter of consciously held beliefs but of the shared practices of our day-to-day lives.

How does all of that relate to Christian formation? That is not an easy question to answer, but we might begin by stressing that it must relate in one way or another. We do not come to formation for Christian vocation as some kind of blank sheet of paper, ready to be written on for the first time; we are more like a bundle of papers that has been scribbled over repeatedly, in different hands, with frequent additions, notes, crossings out and revisions. When we seek to be formed so that we can respond to God's call in Christ, we bring all of that with us. We cannot simply set it aside or disown it, nor should we; 'the quite ordinary course of human growth, development, and life events is the primary instrument of God's shaping, of God's preparing persons for the reign/commonwealth'.[1] Yet neither can we safely assume that all that has shaped us so far and continues to shape us is congruent with God's transforming work in our lives. Some things may need to be undone, or redone; to go back to the analogy, some pages may need to be rewritten or even left behind.

Christian formation, then, always happens in relation to secular formation. Let me try to explain what I mean by that, not least as 'secular' can be a confusing term. First, it can have a relatively neutral sense which reflects its origins in the Latin word *saeculum*, meaning a period of time: in this sense, the secular is just the present 'age', the day-to-day world in which we live at this particular point in human history, with its particular characteristics and circumstances. Second, it can imply an affirmation of the secular in the first sense which excludes any kind of transcendent horizon, and in particular religion. This meaning is bound up with the ideology of secularism. Third, from a Christian perspective, it can be linked to a critique of the secular in the first sense which seeks to discern within it that which belongs to the 'age' of sin and death that needs to end in order for the new age of God's reign to break through. 'Do not be conformed to this world,' Paul writes in Romans 12.2, where 'world' translates the Greek word for 'age'.[2]

In speaking of secular formation, I am primarily invoking the first sense, while also wanting to be alert to both the second

---

1 Robert Davis Hughes III, 2008, *Beloved Dust: Tides of the Spirit in the Christian Life*, New York: Continuum, p. 107.

2 Scriptural quotations are taken from *The Holy Bible Containing the Old and New Testaments: New Revised Standard Version*, 1995, Oxford: Oxford University Press, unless otherwise indicated.

and the third. It is a matter of fact that we are constantly being formed by the day-to-day world in which we live at this particular point in human history, with its particular characteristics and circumstances. To be human is to be, in a famous phrase from the Greek philosopher Aristotle, a 'political animal' – that is, a living being that finds its identity in structured social relationships mediated by cultural forms. We cannot be human without breathing in continually the culture of our society, any more than we can stop breathing in the oxygen in the atmosphere. Christian formation, therefore, cannot be simply about halting or reversing our secular formation. It does however require some discernment as to which aspects of that secular formation in the neutral sense may in fact be binding us to the age of sin and death we have now left behind in Christ. This task is complicated for us in the contemporary context by the way that secularism claims the territory of the secular in the first, neutral sense as its own and seeks to make it inhospitable for religious practice and theological thought. While we need to pay careful attention to such moves, we should not simply concede the ground either.[3]

Secular formation as I have just defined it is a huge topic, and one that would require the expertise of philosophers, historians, psychologists, sociologists and anthropologists to explore fully. The three short chapters that follow in this first part of the book are simply intended to raise awareness of the relevance of this subject for us if we are serious about understanding Christian formation today, and also to be an introduction to some of the critical issues. In particular, it is vital to recognize that our secular formation, with its pervasive messages about human fulfilment, will inevitably slant the way we hear the traditional

---

3 My understanding of the secular here and in the chapters that follow draws on some of the many rich ideas developed in Charles Taylor, 2007, *A Secular Age*, Cambridge, Massachusetts: Belknap Press.

language of Christian vocation, with consequences that may at least appear sharply at odds with that tradition itself.

Each chapter explores a theme in secular formation as I have just defined it which also figures as a critical theme in Christian formation as response to divine vocation: freedom, knowledge and love. These themes separately and together feature in deeply powerful narratives about human fulfilment that we learn not by studying philosophy or history but simply by taking part in the social and cultural world. In order to understand their power in our formation, however, we need to do some history and philosophy, and that is part of my purpose in the following three chapters. Each begins with brief initial reflections on the theme, before the first main section traces some of the historical roots of the narratives of human fulfilment associated with it that are characteristic of modern culture. The second section then takes a closer look at how those narratives appear in the contemporary context and some of the tensions and even contradictions we might identify there. Finally, the third section begins to explore an area relating to the theme of the chapter where we can expect to find significant crosscurrents between secular and Christian formation and opens up issues to be considered in more detail in the remaining parts of the book.

1

Freedom

'For freedom Christ has set us free,' Paul tells the Galatians (Gal. 5.1). God calls us to freedom, and Christian formation, therefore, means growth into freedom. God also calls us in freedom: in divine freedom, we are invited to respond in our human freedom. The deeper and fuller our freedom, the deeper and fuller our 'yes' to the free and gracious call of God. Christian formation, then, is a journey into freedom. To go further in vocation, at any stage of our discipleship, we need to become more free to say yes to all that God is asking of us.

How we hear this message will inevitably be affected by the way our secular formation has shaped our understanding of human freedom and our efforts to achieve it for ourselves and others. That formation arises, first and foremost, from our own life story. Human development in childhood and adolescence is bound up with the experience of various kinds of constraint on our desires and how we react to that. We are likely to perceive as negative the constraints that stand in the way of our conscious desires, and we naturally seek to overcome them: we want freedom from them. What obstacles and limits to our will loomed especially large for us as children and young people? How might our struggles then still configure the way we try to protect and increase our freedom today? What is our response when we feel that our freedom is under threat or somehow blocked? All of this will have an effect on the way we hear about freedom in the context of Christian formation. At a certain point, we may need to take some time to explore the messages we have internalized about freedom from earlier stages of our lives and ask whether they could be standing in the way of the journey into freedom in Christ.

Within our secular formation, however, our unique life story is inseparable from our participation in culture and society. It is through such participation that we learn the word 'freedom' itself, that we are presented with stories for making sense of it and that we acquire ideas we can use to think about what it might require from us in different situations. How our culture frames the idea of freedom, fostering our desires for it and interpreting our identity as persons through it, is the focus of this first chapter. The freedom that Paul was pleading for the Galatians to walk in cannot be straightforwardly identified with the freedom that is celebrated in contemporary society at large. We begin our analysis of secular formation therefore by trying to get to grips with the thinking about freedom that we are bound to bring with us as we seek to be formed for freedom in Christ.

Modern developments: from dependence to autonomy

We are shaped by stories. Human beings know that they are changing, that they can bring change to people and the world around them and that death brings some kind of an end to this process of interaction. Through stories, they make sense of the changes that are happening and articulate direction for the changes that they seek. A story is a representation of change: this is the way things are; this is a path that leads out of it; this is the new place where the path arrives.

We are constantly exposed to stories, articulated and implied, factual and fictional, at work and at play. Within this multiplicity, however, there are some underlying patterns that suggest normative narratives of human fulfilment: this is the way that human beings become what they should be. These narratives are pivotal for our secular formation; they provide the assumptions, for the most part taken for granted, that frame the way we see ourselves, other people and the world around us. And perhaps the most consistently influential narrative of human fulfilment in modern culture is about the transition from dependence to freedom. It appears relatively explicitly in science fiction and fantasy genres where freedom from authority and constraint is shown as decisively separating humans from other beings – most obviously in the contrast with robots and robot-like aliens such as Dr Who's recurring adversaries, the Daleks and the Cybermen. It is prevalent in our politics, where the promise of greater freedom for individuals and societies retains a uniquely compelling attraction. It also figures as a powerful background assumption in the many versions of modern psychology which present autonomy (living by one's own law) as the natural and proper goal of human development. Standard approaches to contemporary bioethics make the first criterion for decisions about medical treatment 'to safeguard individual autonomy'.[4]

Now, freedom has always been a goal for human beings. The question, however, is what we think we need to be free from and what we thereby hope to become free for. Those have not been constants in human history. The idea that dependence on others, and in particular on the authority of others, is necessarily limiting to my freedom has some quite specific origins in Western history. Note that this story about human fulfilment also carries a strong implication about what it means to be a human being: it is to be an individual, whose freedom is

---

4 Cited in R. Kendall Soulen, 2006, 'Cruising toward Bethlehem: Human Dignity and the New Eugenics', in R. Kendall Soulen and Linda Woodhead (eds), *God and Human Dignity*, Grand Rapids, Michigan: Eerdmans, p. 105.

established by resisting the authority of anything or anyone beyond themselves.

This is a characteristically 'modern' story about human beings. While the word 'modern' can mean different things in different contexts, here I mean the period of European history that follows the end of the Middle Ages and the initial flowering of the Renaissance. The sixteenth and seventeenth centuries might be described as 'early' modernity, with the eighteenth seeing its full emergence. The movement known as the Enlightenment is often considered to express some leading ideas of modernity: the supremacy of reason, the questioning of religious and political authority, the exploration of the human world through travel and the natural world through experimental science, and the conscious attempt to establish better, more 'rational' forms of social and political life.

An early articulation of the characteristically modern story of human fulfilment as hinging on transition from dependence to freedom can be seen in the work of Spinoza. Writing in the second half of the seventeenth century, Spinoza took familiar Christian language about bondage and freedom and radically transposed its meaning: for him, religious adherence itself becomes the bondage from which we need to be released in order to become truly free, independent from the control of others. In childhood, we are properly subject to the authority of our parents. In adulthood, the authority of religion, in alliance with the state, improperly tries to control our actions and even our beliefs. It is time, Enlightenment thinkers said, to reject that control and formulate our own beliefs and even our own forms of political life. It is time to grow up.

According to this intensely powerful narrative, the way to human fulfilment is through the rejection of all external authority, beginning with institutional religion. We must refuse to do as we are told and commit ourselves to doing only what we judge to be right, on the basis of our own independent decision-making.

Anything less represents a failure to grow up and live a truly human life. *His Dark Materials*, the trilogy of novels for children and adults by Philip Pullman, represents among other things a sustained contemporary celebration of this message.

Contemporary issues: expressive individualism

The continuing influence of the Enlightenment on our culture is evident in the power of the idea that fulfilment comes from freedom and freedom from the refusal to be dependent on an external authority. But where does it end? From the eighteenth century until the closing decades of the twentieth, there was a succession of competing secularist gospels of human freedom to answer that question, with Marxism being one of the last to wield widespread influence. Since the 1970s, however, such 'grand narratives', as they were labelled in an influential study, have suffered a spectacular collapse in their support. This was presented as grounds for claiming that we were now living in a postmodern time.[5] The idea that we have somehow decisively broken with the trajectory of modernity and moved into a new, postmodern era was widely discussed in the final decades of the twentieth century.[6] Yet while it is undoubtedly the case that a number of very significant shifts were occurring during this period, strong elements of continuity remain. There is therefore a good case for characterizing our age as late modern rather than postmodern. That is the term I use in this book, and in the central section of each of the three chapters in Part 1 a relatively consistent picture should begin to emerge of what we

---

5 Jean-François Lyotard, 1984, *The Postmodern Condition: A Report on Knowledge*, trans. Geoff Bennington and Brian Massumi, Manchester: Manchester University Press.

6 David Harvey, 1990, *The Condition of Postmodernity: An Enquiry into the Origins of Cultural Change*, Cambridge, Massachusetts: Blackwell.

have lost and what we have maintained in the transition to late modernity. In brief, while we no longer have faith in the various gospels of secularist modernity, the characteristic practices of modernity have in many cases continued and even accelerated in their development, and therefore the narratives of human fulfilment communicated by them remain hugely influential for us.

Our secular formation, for instance, still encourages us to see the rejection of authority as fundamental to human flourishing and maturity. At the same time, it also now discourages us from attachment to any strong account of what the goal of a humanity liberated in this way might actually be. Instead, the individual act of autonomous choosing, of deciding without determination by others, has become the defining content of human freedom. Such acts are not 'for' any further goal: rather, they serve as a self-justifying, self-sufficient activity that becomes itself the goal of human living. Hence we talk about a free society as one in which unconstrained choosing happens: where I live, what job I do, which brand of clothing I wear, which political party I vote for.

In the next two chapters, we will be considering how knowledge and love have, in different ways, in fact served to give freedom a purpose in the modern world beyond the mere activity of choice. Yet there is another important point to introduce before we do that. The defining claim of modernity, on one account, is that 'no essential order binds men from the origin to the end of all things.'[7] Our freedom should not be determined by the institutions of family, Church and state because to be human is to be undetermined by the given, by the set rhythms of reality. Instead, to be human is to find and indeed make your

---

7 Anthony J. L. Cascardi, 1992, *The Subject of Modernity*, Cambridge: Cambridge University Press, p. 32. An influential work in articulating this idea was Leo Strauss, 1953, *Natural Right and History*, Chicago: University of Chicago Press.

own place in the world. Via the Romantic movement of the eighteenth and nineteenth centuries this claim generates what the philosopher Charles Taylor calls 'expressive individualism'. The self only exists in its expression and we therefore each have an obligation 'to live up to our originality' – which we must derive from within our unique selves and not by looking to any external or already existing source. It might not be going too far to describe this as the default religion of our time: the duty of what becomes variously known as self-actualization, self-fulfilment or self-realization, and the celebration of whatever people are perceived to do for its sake.[8]

It is surely no accident that this message appears so persuasive in contemporary societies where global capitalism and the technologies it has spawned fill our lives with the spectacle of endless opportunities for free, self-expressive choice. If the popular song that tells us to 'Search for the hero inside yourself' could be an anthem for expressive individualism, its use as a soundtrack for a car advert indicates how that ideology has become bound up with economics. This is partly about consumerism and the multiplication of competing goods and services in so many areas of our lives, partly too about the proliferation of information technologies and how these have intersected with economic behaviour. Glancing at a screen on my desk, my wall or in my hand, I am confronted with a vast range of things to view, interact with and possess. The message of those purveying products will tend to be, more or less: get this thing, and share this identity. But where does this identity come from – surely I must realize it is just a fiction created by the advertising industry, which will spin a new fiction about the same brand in a year's time? If freedom as autonomous choosing is self-validating, it

---

8 Charles Taylor, 1989, *Sources of the Self: The Making of the Modern Identity*, Cambridge, Massachusetts: Harvard University Press, pp. 368–90 (quotation from p. 375); 2007, *A Secular Age*, Cambridge, Massachusetts: Belknap Press, pp. 473–504.

hardly matters. The fiction becomes reality for just as long as I choose to live it. If I express myself by adopting it, it becomes my truth.

The intersection between technology, consumption and imagination is relevant in other ways too. Commentators have written about the relationship between the modern novel and the modern self: fiction, in a book, at the cinema or on television, allows me to imagine different ways of living, different perspectives that are not 'real' but may end up informing how I live my 'real' life in all kinds of ways.[9] The exponential growth of information technology not only gives access to an immense range of images, ideas and stories with ever increasing rapidity, in a way that would have astonished people of just thirty years ago, it increasingly allows me to interact with thousands of 'real' human others but also with virtual contexts that blur the traditional boundaries of fiction and ordinary life. I can become a character in a fiction that I am creating together with others in real time. What is the relationship between my cyber-self and my family-self and work-self? Who is to say that one is more real than the other? Who is to say that one is more truly me than the other?

Here the late modern world reprises the central message of mid-twentieth century Existentialism, another of the 'grand narratives' we have apparently abandoned: you are who you choose to become – not now on the basis of anguished reflection, but in a process of more or less conscious fantasy, in which constant self-reinvention is seen as the desirable goal. If modernity made the self a deliberate 'project' for the first time, late modernity intensifies and fragments that movement.[10] As an influential sociologist comments, 'In our liquid modern

---

9 Cascardi, *Subject*, pp. 72–124.

10 Anthony Elliott, 2007, *Concepts of the Self*, 2nd edn, Cambridge: Polity. Cf. Paul Ricoeur, 1970, *Freud and Philosophy: An Essay on Interpretation*, ET, New Haven: Yale University Press, p. 45.

times, when the free-floating, unencumbered individual is the popular hero, "being fixed" – being "identified" inflexibly and without retreat – gets an increasingly bad press.'[11] The less that binds us, the freer we are to keep constructing new forms of identity and hence become our ever-changing selves. That, at least, is the secular promise.

Crosscurrents in formation: vocation and selfhood

Christian formation needs to provide some kind of context for engaging with these powerful cultural messages about freedom and how it defines our distinctive existence as human beings. This might well include some critical probing of the secular promise of fulfilment through autonomous, self-expressive acts of choice between alternatives. Yet there are aspects of how the theme of freedom figures in our culture that may be convergent with a Christian understanding. Our efforts in Christian formation will be more likely to be productive if we are able to work with the grain of our culture in some respects, rather than engaging in the futile attempt to stop breathing the oxygen of culture that is in fact necessary for human living. For instance, in the Preface I said that the common vocation we all share in Christ is lived out in a unique way by each one of us. I could add that this journey is not mapped in advance, and no one is in a position to tell me exactly how it will progress. That is because vocation is about the meeting of freedoms – God's freedom with ours, my freedom with the freedom of those I serve and serve with and serve under. The unfolding of God's call in a person's life is always an unrepeatable adventure. The formation that takes place as it unfolds will also therefore share this character: being changed in response to God's call is a

---

11 Zygmunt Bauman, 2004, *Identity: Conversations with Benedetto Vecchi*, Cambridge: Polity, p. 29.

voyage of unique discovery, including self-discovery. Such themes are embedded in a theology of creation and humanity, but they are also likely to resonate deeply for people shaped by the secular formation I have been describing. Indeed, it would be self-deceiving to imagine that my own secular formation has not shaped the way I articulate these themes for Christian theology and spirituality.

There are also points, however, where the way secular culture teaches us to understand and practise freedom generates specific tensions for Christian formation. For instance, one of the repeated concerns I pick up in conversation with church leaders in this country is the way that the language of 'my vocation' and 'my ministry' by clergy only serves to confirm that here too 'the desire to live one's own life has become the guiding impulse for people in the Western world'.[12] How can we affirm the response to vocation as always profoundly personal (as it must be, for God addresses us as persons) without rendering it an individual project?

Taylor's concept of expressive individualism can help us to understand at least part of what is happening here. Our society tends to split the institutional and the corporate from the personal, because the personal is defined in terms of the individual self expressing its unique identity through unfettered choices. If we speak about vocation as personal without questioning this cultural framework, our words will be taken to convey the message that vocation is another way – perhaps the ultimate way – for me to express my individual identity. Once that becomes how I see vocation, institutions – represented by church leaders – and even church communities will be cast in the role of means to the end of seeking my goals and making

---

12 H. Russel Botman, 2006, 'Covenantal Anthropology: Integrating Three Contemporary Discourses of Human Dignity', in Soulen and Woodhead (eds), *God and Human Dignity*, p. 77.

my choices in order to 'live my own life'. The frustration by those in positions of institutional authority with such attitudes is, of course, paradoxically only likely to reinforce them by appearing to confirm that the personal and the institutional are unconnected and indeed at a deep level incompatible.

There is no way to break this painful impasse other than by recovering a much richer understanding of human person-hood that allows selves to be at home in relationships, includ-ing those where responsibility and authority are significant parameters, and extending to organizational and institutional life. Otherwise, we oscillate between a merely institutional understanding of vocation as doing what others decide you should do for the good of the organization and a narrowly individual understanding of vocation as doing what I decide I should do for my own self-fulfilment and self-expression. Christian formation will then itself become divided into two halves that can never be whole: learning to conform to the ex-pectations of the organization on the one hand, and pursu-ing my individual journey of spiritual fulfilment on the other. Neither of these sterile alternatives begins to imagine the voca-tion for which Christian formation is fitting us as God's call, a call which comes to persons always for their own sake and always also for the sake of others, and hence is both necessarily personal and necessarily not individual.

Chapter review

The promise of freedom through overcoming dependence on others is close to the heartbeat of modern culture. As a way of understanding human fulfilment, it shapes us through political and economic life as well as through the media and the arts. In the contemporary context, it has become bound up with what Charles Taylor calls 'expressive individualism', the idea that we can and must actualize ourselves through expressing our unique individuality. This makes it difficult for us to talk about Christian formation relating to the person without this being heard as the message that vocation is really about the individual 'living their own life'. If we say it is not about the individual, however, we risk being understood instead as implying that it is all about the institutional Church and conforming to its expectations.

2

Knowledge

In John's Gospel, Jesus makes a series of claims about who he is: the light of the world, the good shepherd, the bread of life. One of these claims is to be the truth (John 14.6), and the celebration of the knowledge of truth that has come to us through Christ is a theme elsewhere in the New Testament as well (e.g. John 8.32; 1 Cor. 1.4–6; Col. 2.1–3). God calls us to know who God is for us and who we are before God, and therefore the journey of Christian formation is a journey into knowledge as well as into freedom. Indeed, the two are inseparable: to say yes to God's call is to say yes to knowing the truth that sets us free.

We are called to knowledge, then, as we are also called to freedom. Here again, however, we need to recognize the extent to which our secular formation in its many dimensions shapes the way we think about knowledge, the way we try to understand things and the place we give to knowing in our account of human identity. As with freedom, our own unique histories will be a decisive part of this. Learning is integral to human development from our earliest beginnings: as children and adolescents, to what extent was it exciting to discover new things, and to what extent was it threatening? When we asked why, did people show patience in explaining problems to us? Did we find their responses baffling or enlightening, encouraging or intimidating? What is the knowledge that we have come to consider precious, and what claims about knowledge are we inclined to dismiss or ignore?

It is also important to reflect here on our specifically educational formation. We will all have participated for many years of our lives in intensive educational processes through which we have learnt not only particular subject areas but also what is worth knowing, how we can come to know it and why we should care about doing so. Such processes most obviously include school, university and professional training. We should not ignore, though, both ongoing education in the workplace and the more informal education we may experience in voluntary contexts. All of these are likely to be powerfully formational, and not simply in terms of what is explicitly taught. Education is also likely to have transmitted to us some of the deep assumptions about knowledge that are a feature of late modern culture – assumptions that need to be identified if they are not to become hidden obstacles as we seek to respond to our Christian vocation by growing in knowledge and understanding.

Modern developments: dare to know

In the *Republic*, the Greek philosopher Plato has Socrates tell a kind of parable about human life as being confined in a cave, watching shadows move across a wall. It is very difficult but not impossible for us to turn round and see the fire that is casting the shadows. Ultimately, however, if our eyes can adjust to its light, we can find our way out of the cave and into the sunshine of the world beyond it.

For Plato, as for his teacher Socrates, the human predicament is characterized by ignorance. We may think we know things, but actually our so-called knowledge is a matter of hazardous guesswork, full of gaps and contradictions. This is the cave in which we appear to be trapped. Yet it is possible to escape and to begin to know the truth. To do this, we must submit to a process of critical reasoning in which our everyday assumptions are questioned and knowledge can be established from its true foundations. We must become philosophers, so that we can begin to live in the real world, the world of unchanging realities and reliable knowledge. It is hard, but not impossible. That is Plato's story about human fulfilment.

You would have to search quite hard in the world today for someone who could be straightforwardly described as a Platonist. Yet in different ways and different combinations, Plato's ideas have been remarkably persistent. The story of human fulfilment as a difficult journey from ignorance to truth requiring commitment to disciplined reasoning recurs in many different contexts, including fictional narratives where it is pivotal for the development of central characters and hence the plot as a whole. The first *Matrix* film would be just one example of this: an insistence on asking questions and seeking answers precipitates the hero's induction into knowledge which turns his world upside down. Ultimately, however, it also enables him to engage with the 'really real' for the first time, recognizing the shadows on the wall for what they are.

A defining feature of much (though not all) Enlightenment thinking from the eighteenth century onwards has been the way it combines this long-standing theme in Western thought with the narrative of freedom from authority we reviewed in the previous chapter. In this perspective, real knowledge means knowledge that is freed from authority, including specifically the authority of tradition. If human beings are defined by their ability to use their independent powers of reason to move from ignorance to truth, then to accept things as true on grounds other than our own process of reasoning here and now is to act in a less than human way. Being properly human means believing only what I can demonstrate is true by reason, just as it means acting on the basis of my own judgement and not in accordance with external authority. Kant summed up the spirit of the Enlightenment with the motto *Sapere aude*: dare to know.

Now, it is generally accepted that it cannot be rationally proved that Jesus was the Son of God or rose from the dead. In that case, some Enlightenment rationalists argued, it has to be less than fully human to hold such non-rational beliefs and therefore they should be rejected in the name of human maturity.

There were strong reactions against the Enlightenment's confidence in human reasoning, from the eighteenth century to the present day. Yet it remains a potent influence. Consider the massive amount of attention and respect given to critiques of religion by the 'new atheists' such as Richard Dawkins, which continue the same line of argument I have just described, though with the difference that now the discipline of rational thinking deemed to be the high road from ignorance to knowledge is not philosophy (as it was for much of the eighteenth and nineteenth centuries) but the natural sciences. For these contemporary representatives of Enlightenment thinking as for their rather distant forebears, it is essentially sub-human to believe what we cannot prove for ourselves through rational thinking. That is what keeps humanity chained in the dark cave of ignorance, from which the 'enlightened' are called to help release it so it may find its true fulfilment.

Contemporary issues: the limits of knowledge

There have always been those who doubted whether rationality can really lead us out from the darkness of the cave. Sceptical voices, from ancient Greece to the present day, have argued that our ignorance cannot be changed: we have no ultimately reliable knowledge about anything. Truth is beyond us.

While the argument between rationalists and sceptics has been carried on throughout the period of modernity, we seem to be living at a time when the doubters can seem to have gained the upper hand. For all the continuing cultural prestige of science, our Victorian forebears who devoted their lives to the accumulation of scholarly and scientific knowledge, to be systematically summarized in ever more comprehensive and truthful editions of the *Encyclopaedia Britannica*, clearly belong to another and increasingly remote age. Relativism as a form of scepticism – the view that since all opinions are relative to a particular context, no view can be objectively true – is fashionable and indeed often expressed (paradoxically) in highly dogmatic terms.

Late modern scepticism is also strongly tinged with a particular kind of cynicism, with roots in the so-called 'masters of suspicion', Nietzsche, Freud and Marx. These writers offered different but potentially complementary ways of interpreting claims to knowledge as disguised attempts at control and power. By presenting all talk about knowledge as motivated by (hidden) desires, they made possible a new level of sophistication in scepticism which has been widely influential at a popular as well as an academic level. Whether you are reading philosophy, psychology or political theory or whether you are eavesdropping in the playground or the pub, you may be able to make out the same basic refrain: 'The reason you're saying that is just because you want to . . .' Unmasking the self-interested motivations behind claims to knowledge is assumed to enable us to dismiss the claims themselves and the truths they pretend to convey. This kind of cynicism gives a perverse kind of moral superiority to sceptics in an age of expressive individualism; by refusing to make any claims about truth, they abstain from the imposition of their own agenda on others, and thus from constraining their freedom of action and expression.

If freedom from authority does not then lead us securely into knowledge, does knowledge necessarily affirm and promote our freedom? The application of characteristically modern forms of rationality to human life itself can seem to subvert modern hopes of freedom by dissolving the reality of free human action. For instance, sciences of the brain and indeed most philosophies of mind assume that for every mental 'event' (including thinking) there exists some kind of corresponding physical event in the brain. But how is this correspondence to be understood? Does my mind 'make things happen' in my brain? That raises very difficult questions about how the non-physical can act on the physical and anyway invokes an understanding of souls as independent from bodies that has been under sustained attack in much philosophy since the seventeenth century. If, however, it is the chemical reactions in my brain that 'make things happen' in my conscious mind, then enlightened knowledge seems to have evacuated the Enlightenment ideal of freedom of all meaning. Freedom is and always will be an illusion. We just follow the chemical script.

The same pattern of secularist knowledge subverting secularist freedom occurs in other contexts as well. Psychology, economics and sociobiology, highly influential in different ways within contemporary Western societies, all present themselves as sciences of the human. All are premised on the assumption that human behaviour is, in broad terms, predictable: humans are motivated by a definable set of factors that can be analysed and used as the basis for making judgements about what they will do in response to particular circumstances. The humans in those circumstances may well believe that they are choosing 'freely', while the scientist knows that they are following a prescribed pattern. The price of scientific knowledge about humanity is the stripping away of our illusions about human freedom as undetermined choosing. Sciences of the human take it for granted that all human behaviour is determined, all the time.

The dilemma here is illustrated particularly acutely in the work of Freud.[13] At various points in his writings, Freud expressed the clear view that modern, scientific knowledge required us to subscribe to determinism, i.e. the view that all human action is

13 W. W. Meissner, 1984, *Psychoanalysis and Religious Experience*, New Haven: Yale University Press; Alasdair MacIntyre, 2004, *The Unconscious: A Conceptual Analysis*, rev. edn, New York: Routledge.

determined by causes that we cannot resist or control. For Freud, we are specifically controlled by the desires of the unconscious, which we are unable to summon for conscious inspection. That is the knowledge to which enlightened reason leads us – and thereby shows us to be puppets on a string, not independent individuals freely making rational choices. Yet Freud gave his life to practising and promoting psychoanalytic therapy on the grounds that it helped people to understand themselves better and thereby acquire greater control – in other words, greater freedom through greater knowledge. Indeed, Freud could not explain the difference between 'normal' and neurotic or psychotic behaviour without defining normal behaviour as relatively free from unconscious childhood influences.

Freud needed the Enlightenment ideal of freedom through independent reasoning to give sense to his life's work, even though he also believed that freedom and therefore personhood is in fact illusory. Rejecting the reality of human personhood left him with an impossible dilemma which, to his credit, he refused to resolve by abandoning his care for human beings. His inconsistency is one example of the way that over the past hundred years many people have come to hold together reductionist views of human existence deriving variously from biology, psychology or sociology on the one hand, and an attachment to such ideals as rights, freedom and dignity on the other, despite the basic contradiction that seems to be involved here.[14]

Crosscurrents in formation: tradition and rationality

As suggested in the previous chapter, Christian formation today requires a discerning approach to themes in secular formation. Some of the ideas we have been considering clearly need to be

---

14 Kevin Vanhoozer, 1997, 'Human Being, Individual and Social', in Colin E. Gunton (ed.), *The Cambridge Companion to Christian Doctrine*, Cambridge: Cambridge University Press, pp. 161–3.

rejected. For instance, the claim that the methods of the natural sciences can be used to achieve a comprehensive and definitive understanding of human beings has been repeatedly made over the past two centuries and continues to require resistance. We can only consider ourselves as exclusively the objects of science by rendering ourselves as physical things and bracketing out any claim about our distinctiveness as persons.[15] In other words, in order to know ourselves wholly through science we must also abolish ourselves, as C. S. Lewis memorably argued.[16] If we are not prepared to do that and instead recognize the incoherence – indeed the irrationality – of such a proposal, then we accept that the limits of natural science are not the limits of our knowledge, and the limits of reality as disclosed by natural science are not the limits of reality as such either.

Such a position is unlikely to be consciously held by someone seeking to be formed in and for their Christian vocation. Yet it is a position that dramatizes in particularly extreme form tensions that are more or less bound to arise for Christian formation in the context of late modernity as it seeks for growth in knowledge. We mentioned in the previous chapter that modernity resists the idea that human beings have a given place in the order of things. Likewise, characteristic approaches to knowledge in modernity assume that what is known as part of that order is unlike those who know it and hence stand somehow outside it, and therefore knowledge requires us to put aside any misleading sense we may have of being related to what we seek to understand. Hence we should place no trust in empathy or intuition – or in tradition when it comes to understanding the past, for tradition cannot place us in any kind of real relationship to history.

---

15 Fraser Watts, 2002, *Theology and Psychology*, Aldershot: Ashgate, p. 4.

16 C. S. Lewis, 1965, *The Abolition of Man or Reflections on Education with Special Reference to the Teaching of English in the Upper Forms of Schools*, New York: Macmillan, pp. 65–91.

It should not therefore be surprising that since the nineteenth century, how to respond to the Enlightenment affirmation of rationality as antagonistic to authority and tradition has been a persistent and at times divisive issue in Christian formation.[17] Can the educational dimension of this in the modern world really be about teachers faithfully passing on to learners the Christian tradition with which both identify, with due warning about deviations from it? Or should it rather be about trying to take off the distorting lenses of traditional perspectives, interrogating evidence and ideas afresh for ourselves and accepting only conclusions that are defensible according to our own rational judgement here and now? Stories about devout believers 'losing their faith' after undertaking theological studies in the context of formation are legion, and they continue to exercise a powerful hold over the imagination of some communities and individuals. Within the ongoing life of the local church, those who have survived such struggles themselves may agonize over the extent to which potentially destabilizing ideas and questions should be shared with the congregation.

Although this is a question that touches on every area of the theological curriculum, in my experience it often comes into particularly sharp focus with biblical studies. Is the meaning of the text something to be learnt from authoritative sources within Christian tradition, or is it only really disclosed by the application of historical methods that bracket out traditional assumptions and may even regard them with active suspicion? Historical-critical approaches to Scripture have to some extent been premised on the assumption that earlier, self-consciously theological traditions of interpretation cannot be trusted: we must figure out what the text means ourselves, on the basis

---

17 Overcoming the opposition between tradition and rationality has been a persistent theme in the work of the philosopher Alasdair MacIntyre, e.g. 1990, *Three Rival Versions of Moral Enquiry: Encyclopaedia, Genealogy, and Tradition*, London: Duckworth.

of the best current historical knowledge, and if such 'secular' historical study undercuts what the Church has always taught, then that teaching is best left to fall away. Conscientious students can end up feeling that they have to choose between the truth of faith that is affirmed through church life and gives them identity and purpose, and the truth of rational knowledge that is presented by academic scholarship and has (apparently) no interest in identity and purpose. Without some hope of negotiation between the two, faith can only be saved by the deliberate repression of thought.

In Chapter 8, we will come back to the question of how we can resist this kind of dilemma and promote a positive and enriching place for growth in understanding as integral to Christian formation. If this is a wrong way of framing the choices, however, this is not to say that there are no choices to be made, or that ultimately we can expect others to make them for us. We do not need to accept Spinoza's views on knowledge and freedom to accept that there is always a kind of growing up involved in understanding, and in particular a taking of responsibility. If I am to come to understand something for myself, I will have to make some decisions about sources, methods and authorities for approaching it. Those who teach in the life of the Church will have to come to their own judgements about different perspectives within Christian theology. They are also likely to have to face at one point or another their own deepest misgivings about the ability of Christian theology itself to give a truthful account of existence. These are arduous tasks that may cost us pain as well as effort, but no one can absolve us of the responsibility involved here without also sentencing us to something less than real understanding. That is where Christian formation does not need to fight secular formation with regard to the search for knowledge – indeed, should not fight it. This is not the same, however, as accepting the Enlightenment ideal of the individual autonomous reasoner, detached from what they are reasoning about. Truth is a gift to us and for us, and a gift that we receive in company with others – not just here and now, but across history as well. To let that truth transform our minds here and now, however, we have to undertake the demanding but also liberating work of growing in understanding. This has to be a vital part of Christian formation today.

Chapter review

Powerful currents in Western modernity have taught that human fulfilment is found in rational knowledge that renounces all dependence on authority or tradition. Only what we can prove here and now to be true without relying on any external testimony should be accepted by mature human beings. While there has been a strong reaction against this kind of rationalism over the past forty years in particular, it remains vibrant in certain contexts (such as the 'new atheism') and continues to shape much of our education and academic life. Although often presented as a message about freedom through knowledge, attempts to apply such thoroughgoing rationalism to human existence itself tend to end by denying the truth of human freedom. All of this means that Christian formation can struggle to affirm the place of thinking in responding to God's call, with serious believers feeling a painful tension between what feeds the heart and what satisfies the head.

3

Love

'God is love' (1 John 4.8) is perhaps one of the most frequently cited statements from the Bible. We are called by the love of God for the love of God, and therefore just as Christian vocation is a journey into freedom and knowledge, so it is also a journey into love. According to another particularly famous passage of the New Testament, anything we may accomplish, no matter how difficult or apparently self-sacrificing, is worthless without love (1 Cor. 13.1–3). It is only with our love that we can begin to respond to the call of God's love. If Christian formation, in any context, is not about the development of our capacity to give and to receive love, it is hard to know what it really has to do with the teaching of the New Testament – however difficult it might be for some educational institutions and indeed the church authorities that oversee them to state this without embarrassment.

As with freedom and knowledge, however, Christian formation has to work with what we bring from our secular formation, sometimes by resisting it, sometimes by accepting it, sometimes by transforming it. The experiences we have of love in our early years inevitably shape us for life, which is not to say that we are merely condemned to repeat them or run away from them. Whatever we hear about love in the context of the Church is bound to be interpreted to some extent through our memories of childhood, both the more and the less easy to recall. Subsequent experiences of love, negative and positive, may provide opportunities for revisiting and indeed healing what is felt to be missing from childhood. Learning how to permit distance and absence within relationships of loving attachment is something that begins before we learn to speak, yet these are also lessons we never decisively master. Sustaining the equilibrium of love is the work of all our lifetimes, and both the fruits and the scars of that work we take with us into Christian formation at every stage.

Our unique history shapes our desire for and understanding of love, but as with knowledge and freedom this history does not happen in a separate space from the unfolding of social and cultural developments. We are bound to interpret our own history in the light of prevailing thinking about human relationships and how people grow into fulfilment and maturity. Moreover, the way we internalize and act out that thinking in our own practice of relating to others will in turn have a profound impact on our lives and the lives of those affected by us.

We have spent two chapters considering how the search for freedom and knowledge gives sense to human living, but for many and indeed perhaps most people, the most important quest is for love. This is the story of human fulfilment that is really compelling at all levels of society. That may seem too obvious to need saying. As in the first chapter we tried to tease out what might be specific to our particular secular formation in the way that we encounter the theme of freedom, so here I want to ask what is distinctive about love in our context and how it affects the ways in which we imagine the human condition and think about human transformation.

Modern developments: romance and the novel

The story of human fulfilment through the drama of romance is all pervasive across our culture: seeing another person, falling in love, developing a relationship, suffering various crises, and finally achieving some kind of fulfilment – or else failing to do that, so the cycle must begin again. It is the staple diet of the popular song and if not always the major theme of a novel, film or play, it is rarely entirely absent. It would be hard to watch a soap opera or sequence of TV advertisements for very long without encountering it. It would seem that we can never weary of its telling.

Now, tales of romantic love are as old as human civilization. The idea that for each person there is some special other person, unity with whom will bring fulfilment, runs very deep. We find it in Plato's *Symposium*, from the fourth century BC, where Aristophanes tells the story of how human beings were originally created by the gods with four arms, four legs, two faces and so on, only to be tragically divided. Hence we have such a deep-seated desire to be reunited with our original other half and cannot rest until we find them. Socrates, however – and through his voice, Plato – relates an alternative myth of love's origins that asserts it can never find a satisfactory conclusion with another human being. Instead, we must become lovers of wisdom (which is what the Greek word from which we get our 'philosopher' originally meant) who turn away from the transient to seek the eternal.

To understand our own expectations about romantic love and its power to determine what we mean by love itself, we might begin with the rise of the modern novel, a genre of writing which became increasingly popular through the eighteenth and nineteenth centuries. Unlike the epic poems and histories that fed the imaginations of the ancient and medieval worlds, the modern novel brackets transcendence. It aspires to the representation of the ordinary, avoiding the heroic and the miraculous, and its characters seek their satisfaction in their relationships with one another.[18] So this is very far from the world of Plato's love. The

18 Ian P. Watt, 1957, *The Rise of the Novel: Studies in Defoe, Richardson and Fielding*, London: Chatto and Windus.

genre of the novel is shaped by the hope that finding the special one is indeed possible, that the quest for love can come to a happy end if only the right partner is found – and married.

Indeed, we might say that marriage comes to symbolize for modernity the potential 'settling' of love not just in a lifelong partnership but in a stable place within society that supports and fosters it. Just as much as eighteenth- and nineteenth-century philosophy seem clear about what freedom and knowledge look like, so many eighteenth- and nineteenth-century novels appear certain as to what love looks like when fully achieved. Human happiness begins when we summon the courage to refuse to allow authority and convention to dictate to us whom we will marry and instead let ourselves be led by love as passionate feeling.[19] Marriage becomes a symbol of how the sharing of such feelings between two people can become the fulfilment of individual freedom won from the battle with enslaving dependence.

The previous chapter reflected on the way that rational knowledge provided one way of answering the question we puzzled over in Chapter 1: what is freedom for? 'Romantic' novels and the mentality they both reflect and promote convey another answer to the same question, contrasting but equally powerful. Release from dependence on external authority and the consequent attaining of human maturity create a space of freedom in which we may find love with another in a relationship of relative equality and mutuality coloured by powerful affections: I choose you, you choose me. They also, however, suggest a basic situation of alienation, escape from which must initially lead us into isolation: we begin trapped in a web of false and suffocating relationships defined by convention, authority and tradition, from which freedom calls us out. Love is then something we discover out of the solitude of freedom.

---

19 Cf. Jean-Claude Kaufmann, 2011, *The Curious History of Love*, ET, Cambridge: Polity, pp. 78–108.

Contemporary issues: unstable relationships

At this point, we return to one of the themes that has emerged from the previous two chapters, the alienation of the modern self from the world in which it exists. Modern freedom means making a place for ourselves, and not accepting that our place is grounded in the order of things. Modern knowledge means reckoning with a reality that is separated from us and indifferent to us. Similarly, modern love means detaching ourselves from the given relationships that hem us in (such as family and social status), realizing that our basic situation is that of autonomous individuals and then following the choices of our heart to create new relationships that are truly ours. We are homeless until we make a home for ourselves; but such a home is inevitably fragile, because it is not anchored in stable patterns of social and cosmic belonging. We are always in danger of falling back into the isolation from which the romantic love of individual, passionate choice alone can rescue us.

In the previous two chapters, late modernity has been shown to be characterized both by a lack of confidence in the goals of modernity and by a continuing adherence to modernity's characteristic themes and practices. The promise of happiness in our society is still carried to a large extent by the hope for relationships that combine erotic intimacy with stable companionship. What has perhaps most obviously changed since the romantic fiction of the eighteenth and nineteenth centuries is that we have a more varied set of expectations about what that might look like and less confidence that once established it will last for a lifetime. The 'relationship revolution' of the twentieth century has changed things here profoundly.[20] 'Happily ever after' no longer means husband and wife moving into preordained

---

20 Duncan J. Dormor, 1992, *The Relationship Revolution: Cohabitation, Marriage and Divorce in Contemporary Europe*, London: One Plus One.

roles within the public and domestic worlds. Social acceptance of contraception, women working outside the home, divorce and remarriage and gay and lesbian lifestyles have left us able to imagine possibilities for romantic and erotic fulfilment (and indeed frustration) very different from those that inspired the producers and consumers of the pre-twentieth-century popular novel.

In the previous section of the chapter, I tried to explain how the story of modern love is bound up with the story of modern attitudes to freedom. If nothing I do can be really *mine* unless it is done freely – in the sense of independently and without authorization by others – then the only kind of relationship that can really express my identity is one that I choose for myself. Love must be free, and that which is presented to me by others does not involve the exercise of my freedom. Hence taking on social roles and responsibilities established by others cannot really be a way of loving, because it cannot be a gesture of freedom as our culture understands it. Doing what I believe to be a duty may be laudable and indeed attract widespread social approval, but it seems strange in our age to talk about it as a form of love.

Even in the mid-twentieth century, it was possible to celebrate love of the 'brotherhood of man' as something to be demonstrated in loyal service to communities and in devotion to causes of social progress. The gap, however, between duty and love in our own time is so wide that it is difficult to find any way across it. Law, duty and loyalty stand on one side of the divide; love, choice and intimacy stand on the other. As what happens in the public realm seems quite cut off from the 'personal' world of my own freedom, and older notions of stability and commitment are stripped out of the experience of work in contemporary capitalism, so expectations about human fulfilment become ever more exclusively focused on intimate relationships and on the space of home and family that we hope to grow around them.[21] These relationships become the primary compensation for the fragmentation and impersonality of our social experience, the only context for relating that holds out the promise of love and belonging in freedom, as opposed to indifferent coexistence and continual competition for resources.

How safe is this kind of love, however, from the forces that make the wider social context so loveless? That wider context fosters the acceptance of something like the philosophical position known as egoism as a guiding principle for interpreting human behaviour. Egoism teaches that self-interest is the one real motivation for everything that we do. As well as featuring widely in philosophy and the social sciences, egoism is served up as the popular wisdom of our age which promises to lay bare the real story about human beings: the 'bottom line' of everyone's behaviour is their own interest, and therefore the only way to manage relationships between individuals, communities or within society is to create some kind of level playing field for the inevitable competition of my interest against yours. The reality of human life is of individuals trying to get what they want either with others or without them, and the way to get what you want is to face up to it. Such apparently 'realistic' thinking feeds directly into both defensive individualism and the kind of cynicism about people and their motivations that we discussed in the previous chapter.

If egoism is true, however, then love, like freedom, is in danger of being unmasked as unreal. I may say – to myself as well as to you – that I love you, but in my dealings with you as in everything else that I do I am actually seeking only what I really want. Being with you may bring me pleasure, but

---

21 Richard Sennett, 1998, *The Corrosion of Character: The Personal Consequences of Work in the New Capitalism*, New York: Norton; Sara Savage, Sylvia Collins-Mayo and Bob Mayo with Graham Cray, 2006, *Making Sense of Generation Y: The World View of 15–25 Year Olds*, London: Church House Publishing.

what ultimately I love is not you at all but my own satisfaction, which you for the time being help me to achieve. When you no longer do that, the pleasant illusion of my love will start to fade and either I will have to find a way to suppress my own wishes in order to stay with you, or I will leave you to discover a new context for their satisfaction. Indeed, egoism can have a corresponding kind of ethics according to which it would actually be wrong for me to make a commitment to another person which might involve ceasing to be faithful to the 'truth' of my own self-interest. Authenticity dictates that I always follow my desires, with the sober knowledge that the only real love is self-love.

Crosscurrents in formation: love and duty

Because of the centrality of love for Christian formation, there is a need to be particularly attentive to strands in our culture that would drain reality from love between persons. Any approach that reduces human motivation without remainder to self-interest – however that interest is defined – renders love between persons an illusion. It must translate the sensation of love for another person into love of the benefit they bring to me. This is a particularly important point because of the presence of versions of egoism within various forms of social science, which those involved in formal training programmes related to Christian formation are more or less bound to encounter. There can be an important corrective for Christians to over-spiritualizing assumptions here: it may be true that whenever I 'feel' love for another person, appreciation of how they benefit me – how the experience of them meets my needs and desires – is part of the picture. Acknowledging and understanding my own interest in relationships that I prefer to frame in terms of selfless love and service might even be crucial for growth in discipleship and ministry at a certain point. But that is not the same as saying that there is nothing moving me in those relationships beyond my own interest.

The disjunction between duty and love represents a deeper and potentially more complex challenge for Christian vocation and therefore formation. Just as our secular formation encourages us to equate persons with individuals and oppose them to institutions, so it also teaches us to equate love with passionately chosen relationships and oppose it to ideas such as duty, service and responsibility. This may partly explain why forms of worship that allow the enactment of the encounter with God in terms of mutual declarations of love and the overflowing of affection arising from this seem able to draw those left cold by much traditional Christianity. I have no wish to disparage this kind of corporate spirituality, but precisely because it gains strength from its affinity with contemporary culture, so it is also exposed to some of its weaknesses. In particular, spiritual-like secular romanticism can flip over into egoism: what I really love is not the other, but the gratification I experience through ecstatic feelings of loving and being loved. Therefore I would rather keep pursuing such experiences than patiently attend to the other I claim to love and what they may actually be asking from me.

The identification of love with ecstatic emotion and intimate relationship may also be part of the reason for the reluctance I mentioned at the start of the chapter to talk frankly about Christian formation as growth in love. Such reluctance, however, only colludes with the separation of individual from relation, freedom from responsibility and love from duty. Christian formation has to find ways to resist this, because we are called to follow the law of love. Love is freedom, but love is also duty that binds us; love is joyful discovery, but love is also faithful service and stubborn commitment. Love of God is attending to God's call of love and desiring above all things to respond to that call with our whole being, whatever kind of experiences we may have or indeed not have as a result.

The new commandment is to love one another as we have been loved by God, in faithfulness and self-giving: love the ordinary, actual people who share worship and fellowship with you. We do not get to choose whom we love in following the call of Christ. They are given to us, and we are called to go on loving them however they may behave and however unlovely they may sometimes appear. The gospel does not call us to participate in a repeating drama of searching for intoxicating love, but in a sustained practice of doing love, day by day, week by week, in the hospitable community of the Church so that the world may begin to know how profoundly and utterly it is loved by God. Christian formation has to be about being changed from the roots of our being in and for that vocation. While we will focus on this again in the very last chapter of the book, it will also be a vital ingredient in everything that follows.

Chapter review

The novel helped to popularize a vision of romantic love in which modern individuals freely choose a relationship that through marriage also secures their place in society. The rise of expressive individualism coincides with a greater openness to pluralism and experimentation in sexual relationships and a distrust of preordained social roles. At the same time, many of our dominant ways of interpreting human activity presuppose a fundamental egoism – the idea that what we do is always at root a matter of seeking our own interest, however that is defined. If this 'reasoning' is correct, love, like freedom in the previous chapter, turns into an illusion: however fervently we think we love another, it is really our own benefit we are seeking and therefore ourselves we are really loving. Christian formation must affirm the reality and goodness of growth in love, as well as freedom and knowledge, yet it also needs to untangle the meaning of love so that it is not at odds with duty, commitment and an acceptance of those given to us as our responsibility: our neighbours, and our sisters and brothers in the body of Christ.

PART 2

Understanding Christian Vocation

In exploring some themes in secular formation in the first part of this book, I tried to show how Christian formation always takes place within the context of our being shaped by continual participation in the present age. The most significant challenges here are not necessarily from those aspects of the secular readily associated with ideological secularism, but from more diffuse currents that drag in subtle but pervasive ways against the positioning of traditional Christianity. Christian formation today requires from us a willingness to reflect carefully on when we may move to some extent at least with these pressures and when we need to find strength to stand against them.

To begin to do that, we need to come back to the question of just what Christian formation is. My starting point has been that Christian formation is how we are shaped in and for vocation, by our response to the call of God. Secular formation arises from all kinds of different interactions, but Christian formation is about the meeting of human persons with God in Christ, a meeting that can be characterized in terms of call: speaking that names us as persons, summons us to action and invites us into an unfolding conversation. If that is right, then in order to think carefully about Christian formation, we need to do some work in understanding Christian vocation. A grasp of the theology of vocation can help us to find stable footing for the demanding tasks of theological discernment that arise from serious engagement with Christian formation in any context and at any level.

Hence the focus for the second part of the book. Although it is somewhat longer that the first, let me stress that it is an exploration of the theology of vocation to help us in understanding formation, and not a comprehensive treatment.[22] As in the first part, this is a complex subject that touches on a wide diversity of different disciplines, though in this case within Christian theology: most notably theological anthropology, but also Christology, pneumatology, ecclesiology and spirituality, and a variety of areas of specialization within each of these. Indeed, there is perhaps no area of Christian theology to which the theology of vocation does not relate at some level. This makes writing about it difficult, but it also highlights why the subject is so critical. For without some kind of integrating reflection on vocation, we are likely to struggle to relate the different strands in our learning for discipleship and ministry to the work of Christian formation.

Creation is the focus for the first chapter in this part of the book. Vocation begins with creation, with God's address to creation as a whole and with God's specific address to humankind. Humanity is called into particular forms of relationship, and there is a corresponding creaturely formation that takes place as we respond to that calling. Yet it is also the case that there is something flawed and broken in our response, so that such formation is always proceeding crookedly; despite the creator's vocation to life, we head towards death.

Chapter 5 then considers how our vocation is renewed through Christ. The eternal Word of God's call became flesh

---

22 For a notable attempt towards this, see L M. Rulla, 1986, *Anthropology of the Christian Vocation*, Vol. 1, *Interdisciplinary Bases*, Rome: Gregorian University Press.

and dwelt among us. In him, the call is heard as good news that confirms God's promises from creation onwards and transforms our situation here and now. Jesus bears God's call and communicates it to us, while he also hears God's call himself and is formed in his response. As the first Christians begin to recognize in Jesus God's eternal Son and the image in whom we are made, so they glimpse the beginning and end of our vocation in the divine communion of the Trinity.

How do we respond to God's call to humanity through Christ? Chapter 6 examines how our shared response within the communion of the Church finds its pattern in the sacraments of baptism and Eucharist. Here our answer to God's call is at once expressed, summed up and made real. The reality of God's grace in the sacraments, however, wants to flow into the whole of our lives, enabling us to respond with our whole being to the summons in the beginning to life in the image of God, to the invitation to communion with the Trinity through the Son and to the call to follow Jesus of Nazareth day by day. As we do this in work, relationships and ministry, we may recognize that our response is to be framed by what I referred to in the Preface as distinctive vocations, of one kind or another. In such cases, they also have a decisive influence on our formation. Nonetheless, vocation and formation in all their various manifestations lead back to the overarching purpose of our calling: being conformed to the image of God's Son.

4

Called in Creation

The theology of vocation is not simply about what happens to some individuals in the life of the Church. It extends to all reality. In the beginning, according to the first chapter of Genesis, there was 'formless void' until God begins to speak (Gen. 1.1–3). God calls creation into existence, in an act of divine freedom, and then calls each thing by name. God calls all creation into existence, but only humanity, in the biblical account, is also able to speak and even speak back to God. The uniqueness of human beings in this account is for the sake of all creation. In our freely being called into life and being able freely to respond to the one who calls us and names us, we enable created reality to fulfil its purpose and receive the fullness of the creator's blessing. The human being 'does not merely *have*' but '*is* a vocation'.[23] To be human is to be addressed by God and to be forever being shaped by this divine summons. Therefore any profound reflection on vocation has to draw us towards the relationship between particular tasks, specific responsibilities, present choices here and now and the call that is the ground of our being, the vocation which we *are* and always will be.

---

23 Henri de Lubac, 1987, *Paradoxes of Faith*, ET, San Francisco: Ignatius, p. 59 (italics in original). See also Kevin Vanhoozer, 1997, 'Human Being, Individual and Social', in Colin E. Gunton (ed.), *The Cambridge Companion to Christian Doctrine*, Cambridge: Cambridge University Press, pp. 183–4.

In the chapter that follows, we begin by reflecting on the account of humanity's creation in the opening pages of the Bible. These pages present humanity in the context of the whole work of God's creation. Men and women are creatures among the multiplicity of creatures, and they belong within that multiplicity in God's good creation. Yet they are also unique creatures, different from all others. They are called into unique relationship with the rest of the creatures on earth, unique relationship between themselves and unique relationship with God. We will take some time to look at each of these in turn. It is in the way that they become woven together, however, that we can best make sense of the scriptural teaching of humanity's creation in the image of God.

The book of Genesis also asserts that something has gone wrong in these relations that characterize humanity, beginning from the relationship between God and humanity and spreading out to affect all our other relationships. Our ability both to hear and to respond to the vocation we have been given as human creatures is impaired and marked by the shadows of sin – pain, domination, struggle and death. Yet God does not cease to call us and human beings do not cease to respond, and in that response formation continues that corresponds amidst the flaws and failings to God's good purpose in the beginning.

Called into relation with the earth

One phrase has a critical role in Genesis 1 for describing the uniqueness of humanity within creation: 'Then God said, "Let us make humankind in our image, according to our likeness . . ."' (Gen. 1.26–27; cf. also 5.1–3 and 9.6). For more than two millennia, these verses have provoked extensive attention and divergent views from biblical interpreters, both Jewish and Christian. Ancient and modern commentators alike have been aware that the introduction of the phrase 'image of God' is followed immediately by the command to human beings to 'have dominion over' all other living things on the earth (Gen. 1.26–28). The narrative of Genesis 1, with its poetic overview of God's work in creating, locates humanity firmly within the diversity of creation and appears to express the uniqueness of humanity initially in terms of ruling over fish, birds, animals and plants.[24]

This might seem an odd place to start in describing the uniqueness of human beings, yet the writers of the Old Testament were clearly struck by the many ways in which human beings can shape the world around them, and in particular the existence of other living things. We have been given a very particular kind of power on earth, and one that they could not help but consider in the light of God's incommensurably greater power as creator (Psalm 8). Today, we tend to be uncomfortable about affirming human power as a positive dimension of God's gift to us. One reason for that is our awareness of the harm we have done, are doing and will continue to do with regard to the living things with which we share this fragile planet. A much-debated article some years ago suggested that these verses from Genesis were in fact at the root of the contemporary ecological crisis, because they had given Western societies influenced by Christianity a licence to exploit the non-human environment with no consideration for its inherent value or well-being.[25]

Many scholars would argue that this represents a serious misreading of Genesis 1 and related biblical texts, in which

---

24 Marc Cortez, 2010, *Theological Anthropology: A Guide for the Perplexed*, London: T. & T. Clark, pp. 21–4. For a detailed theological study of this scriptural motif, see Stanley J. Grenz, 2001, *The Social God and the Relational Self: A Trinitarian Theology of the* Imago Dei, Louisville, Kentucky : Westminster John Knox.

25 Lynn White, 1967, 'The Historical Roots of our Ecologic Crisis', *Science* 155, pp. 1203–7.

dominion and rule need to be understood in terms of the concept of kingship familiar to Old Testament culture, where the king is responsible for the wise stewardship of land, people and resources. (Think about how often the ruler is compared to a shepherd in the Old Testament, for instance, and the judgement that befalls those who fail to care for their sheep, as in Ezekiel 34.1–10.) We might add that the God in whose image humanity is created in Genesis 1 never seeks to use the world he has created in any way at all but simply affirms its goodness and blesses the day in which he rests from his work. Accepting that we are indeed uniquely powerful in relation to every other creature on earth and taking responsibility for the good order of the non-human environment on God's behalf would seem to be how human beings should live out the call to 'have dominion' on this basis. Human beings, then, are called to exercise a unique relation of responsibility for the earth as a whole as one aspect of what it means for them to be made in the image of God.

We might also want to allow Genesis 2 to guide us in our understanding of the call to be fruitful, multiply, fill the earth and have dominion over its creatures in Genesis 1.28. Many modern commentators have thought that from Genesis 2.4 to the end of Chapter 3, we are reading a second account of the creation that may have originally circulated separately from the account in Chapter 1 – though some would disagree. From our point of view, what is most important here is the different emphasis in the two accounts with regard to human creatures. To begin with, in Genesis 2 the plants and the animals are created after, not before, the human creature, and they are created for its sake. The human creature is at the centre in the second creation account: everything else happens in relation to it. In the first creation account, human beings are added as the final, crowning touch to a created order that had already come into being and had its own inherent dynamism (hence perhaps the need for humanity to exercise an active dominion).

Yet there is also a profound convergence between the two stories, in that human creatures are characterized in both by responsibility for non-human creation. In Genesis 2, God puts Adam in charge of the garden of Eden, in a way that parallels the command to have dominion over the whole earth in Genesis 1. In terms of the plants and trees, this means the beginning of agriculture: Adam is placed 'in the garden of Eden to till it and keep it' (Gen. 2.15). Read side by side, the two stories indicate that having dominion means taking responsibility for tending and supervising. It means work aimed at nurturing the earth's potential for life.

The parallels and differences between what Adam does for the plant life of the garden and what he does for its animals are important. When God creates the animals, he brings them to Adam to be named (Gen. 2.19–20) – to set the animal creation in some kind of linguistic order which is also an order for understanding and for activity. Human beings do not have God's power to call beings into existence by speaking, yet they share in the creator's likeness in calling by name what is already there: to interpret what has been made and creatively decide how it will be represented, how it will be called. The uniqueness of humanity's relationship to other earth creatures in the beginning is about power exercised as responsibility, which requires both the work of tending and nurturing and the activity of naming and interpreting. We might say humanity is distinguished from all other creatures on earth by its calling to keep weaving order, consciously and creatively, for the common good of the whole earth.

Called into relation with one another

Although Adam shows his likeness to the creator in naming the animals he meets, none of them is a fitting 'helper' for him. Is this in part because, while he can speak to them, they cannot address him in return? The gift of language can only be received in a community of language. Being human expresses itself in being able to say 'I'. But 'I' implies 'you', and a human 'I' implies a human 'you'. The decree of the Second Vatican Council (1962–65) of the Roman Catholic Church that particularly deals with the theological understanding of the human person expresses the fundamental insight here with a helpful paradox: 'For by his innermost nature man is a social being, and unless he relates himself to others he can neither live nor develop his potential.'[26] We cannot separate what is most 'inward' about ourselves from our being in relation to others.

Until there is man and woman, male and female, and therefore a relationship of inter-human address, the human creation is radically defective in Genesis 2. So long as there is just one human being, humanity is not fully created. *Adam*, the creature that God has fashioned from the ground (*adamah* in Hebrew), needs to be separated into *ish* (man/husband) and *ishshah* (woman/wife) so that humanity can truly come into being through address between human persons (Gen. 2.23). Human existence needs plurality and relationality, with the fundamental form of this being the distinction between men and women. Contrary to millennia of (male) biblical interpretation, there is in fact no male without female, no man without woman (as Paul makes clear in 1 Cor. 11.11–12).

These important themes have led a number of theologians, following the lead of Karl Barth in particular, to argue that the image of God should be understood primarily in terms of

---

26 Vatican II, 1965, 'Pastoral Constitution on the Church in the Modern World: *Gaudium et spes*', www.vatican.va/archive/hist_councils/ii_vatican_council/documents/vat-ii_cons_19651207_gaudium-et-spes_en.html, section 12.

relationship between persons.[27] While this is often presented as an alternative to the view of the image considered in the previous section, that does not seem to me either necessary or helpful. Rather, in both cases the uniqueness of human beings in their relationships speaks of the creator. As human beings have a unique calling to work and responsibility in relation to the earth, so they also have a unique calling to love and delight in relation to one another, and indeed to delight in their working together and to take responsibility in their love for one another.

'Therefore a man leaves his father and his mother and clings to his wife, and they become one flesh' (Gen. 2.24). Human love requires a difficult interplay between union and separation: in order for Adam and Eve to be united in love, the earth creature must be divided via some difficult divine surgery; in order for a man to cling to his wife and the two to become one flesh, he must leave his father and mother. Some kind of deeper separation is necessary in order to enable a more free, more knowing and therefore more intimately loving union. Only by facing the other from the outside, as it were, can we see another human face and recognize this other as one like me: not the same as me, but not my enemy; calling for my attention, my understanding and my love, not bound to overwhelm and absorb me unless I overwhelm and absorb them first.

This ability to endure the 'space between' myself and another and cultivate it with loving regard is how human persons exist and flourish in their selfhood. To become a human self, we have to address and be addressed by a human other; we need to recognize and be recognized by another human person. In

27 Alistair I. McFadyen, 1990, *The Call to Personhood: A Christian Theory of the Individual in Social Relationships*, Cambridge: Cambridge University Press, pp. 17–44; Christoph Schwöbel, 1991, 'Human Being as Relational Being: Twelve Theses for a Christian Anthropology', in Christoph Schwöbel and Colin E. Gunton (eds), *Persons, Divine and Human: King's College Essays in Theological Anthropology*, Edinburgh: T. & T. Clark, pp. 141–65.

creation, we are called into relations of knowledge, freedom and love with other human persons, and this is intrinsic to our humanity. If that is right, it is only in calling and being called by one another that we can begin to respond to the call of our creator. Theologically speaking, therefore, there is no such thing as an 'individual' relationship with God. We know God in and with one another.

Which other? The narrative of Genesis 2 points in two directions which may seem different but which in fact converge. The first direction is a celebration of the exclusive and intimate relation of two persons becoming 'one flesh' through marriage. The second is an affirmation of the inclusive and universal relation of solidarity between all human persons as members of a single human family. We do not need to believe that there was a pair of human individuals who once existed and became parents to the entire human race to see here two significant and complementary truths. It is through an unconditional commitment of freedom to mutual knowing and loving with a particular other person that we discover the mystery of human personhood. Yet the mystery that we discover there is one that we cannot deny to any human person; indeed, as mystery it is a reality in which we participate without being able to comprehend it because we are ourselves comprehended by it, and not a concept that we can apply as we wish. The mystery of any one human person draws us into the mystery of the unity of all human persons, across time and space. Ultimately, just as there is no strictly individual response to God's call, so there is no response that is not somehow with and for the whole human race.

Called into relation with God

In the Scriptures, the mystery of human relating is situated within the primary mystery of the human–divine relationship.

The human creature alone can say 'you' not just to animals and other human beings but to the creator who calls all things into being. The human creature can uniquely answer the creator's call and indeed call on the creator in return. The address of the creator to humanity does not finish with the original calling into being: this is only the beginning of a conversation which has no end. It is this unique relation to God and God's call that is both ground and goal of all the other relations in which human beings participate.[28] Thus it was normal in traditional theology to claim, as Augustine did, that the characteristics of human beings that rendered them creatures in the image of the creator needed to be turned towards the creator for that image to be truly realized. The image is manifested in human relation to God being expressed in human relating to the earth and to one another that corresponds to God's likeness, and these activities being offered back to God their source in thanks and prayer.

The second creation account presents the intimacy between God and human beings in a very striking way. The first human creature, like the first animals, is formed from the ground, but uniquely God 'breathed into his nostrils the breath of life' (Gen. 2.7). He creates a special garden for him to live in, full of trees that are 'pleasant to the sight and good for food' (Gen. 2.9). He gives him specific guidance – the command not to eat the fruit of the tree of the knowledge of good and evil – explains why it is so important and then trusts him to keep it (Gen. 2.16–17). He worries about the loneliness of the human creature and, when his first attempt to overcome this fails, he separates the first human creature to create man and woman (Gen. 2.21–23). Together, they evidently become used to meeting God 'walking in the garden at the time of evening breeze' (Gen. 3.8). This is

---

28 On the relationship between image and call, see John D. Zizioulas, 2006, *Communion and Otherness: Further Studies in Personhood and the Church*, ed. Paul McPartlan, London: T. & T. Clark, pp. 39–43.

the kind of relationship that God intended with humanity, in the beginning.

This unique and intimate relationship, however, is premised on humanity's willingness to accept it as God's gift. 'You may eat freely of every tree of the garden; but of the tree of the knowledge of good and evil you shall not eat, for in the day that you eat of it you shall die' (Gen. 2.16b–17). The gift of the divine command is also the gift of human freedom in relationship with God, however paradoxical that may sound. To ask someone to do something is to acknowledge that they may, in fact, not do it. That God gives Adam a command characterizes Adam as a free creature who can say 'Yes' or 'No' to God. It creates a space for practising acceptance and trust. Like the separation of man and woman, the command is a way of establishing distance to be filled by freedom, knowledge and love, this time between God and humanity, which we may sum up in biblical language as faith. God's command is to be received with joy, as an opportunity to express love for the one who has loved us and given us all things – as is so memorably celebrated in Psalm 119. Faith is how we receive God's address spoken to us and thereby become freely, knowingly and lovingly more fully what we are as God's beloved creatures: 'Faith is not to be ranked by the side of the other faculties in a federation of rival powers, but is behind them all.'[29]

Yet in the beginning, this is not what transpires. Rather than eliciting trust and delight in showing trust, the command becomes the occasion for suspicion, and a shadow falls across God's good creation for the first time. The appearance of evil in the world that God created for good means that the response of humanity to God's call cannot move in a straightforward

---

29 Henry Scott Holland, 1904, 'Faith', in Charles Gore (ed.), *Lux Mundi: A Series of Studies in the Religion of the Incarnation*, 10th edn, London: John Murray, p. 15.

way towards its completion. God's words to the woman and the man in Genesis 3.16–19 speak of pain, domination, struggle and death as realities that they must now face for the first time. These realities confront them as shadows cast by their sin that haunt them and ultimately consume them. They distort and darken human ability to live out creation's call to fill the earth so as to bring peace and order, to dwell with one another in love and justice and to keep company with God in the attentiveness of constant faith. Death marks an end to each human person and thus leaves a widening void in the fragile fabric of human relations. Yet if the response to God's call is radically impaired, does God cease to call us, and do we become incapable of any kind of affirmative response?

Formation as human creatures

In part, our answer to the question I have just posed will depend on how we understand the Christian doctrine of creation. If we understand it as narrating an event that took place at the beginning of history, we may well struggle to see how what the Bible says about creation has any direct bearing on our own experience in the here and now. If, on the other hand, we understand creation as describing that relationship between God and the world which is the ultimate answer to why the world is, then to read Genesis 1—3 as an account of human creation is to receive it as a story that illuminates what it means to be human before God today. And what it tells us is that to be human creatures is to be both addressed by God and incapable of saying 'yes' to that address in a straightforward way. We are therefore always being drawn into formation as human creatures by God's call and also always resisting it.

The vocation to human creatures 'in the beginning' was one that drew them forward into a future of growth and change. It is important to emphasize this because the dominant view for much of the history of Christian theology has been that in the beginning, everything was perfect. The approach I have been taking so far does not accept that view, not least because it does not seem to me to correspond with the biblical witness, beginning with the perspective of Genesis itself. Perhaps it depends on what we mean by 'perfect'. Was the human story meant to come to an end on the very first day of humanity's creation, because then things were exactly as God desired? Surely not: 'Be fruitful and multiply, and fill the earth and subdue it' is God's first command to men and women in the Bible (Gen. 1.28). That sixth day of creation and first day of human life marks the beginning of a story, the space for the adventure of human understanding, freedom and love. That adventure is what defines humanity – what makes us human. We are, to use a technical term in modern philosophy and theology, self-transcending: we can become conscious of the present limits to our knowledge, our freedom and our love and seek to go beyond them, to transcend them and thereby transcend ourselves as we are now.[30] The earth creature was never intended to sit for ever in self-contented pleasure within the protection of the garden of Eden. On the other hand, as soon as this adventure began unfolding, things started to go wrong. It was a perfect beginning, we might say, but it was only ever the beginning, not the end.

The thinking of the great Christian theologian of the second century, Irenaeus of Lyons, can be helpful to us here. Irenaeus taught that Adam was created as a child, intended by God to grow and develop. This is in contrast with what later became the mainstream position in Christian theology that Adam was created perfect and lacking in nothing. Moreover, according to Irenaeus, God always intended that in due course Adam and

---

30 John Macquarrie, 1982, *In Search of Humanity: A Theological and Philosophical Approach*, London: SCM, pp. 25–37.

Eve should proceed to the knowledge of good and evil and to the wisdom that went with it; hence the placing of the tree in the garden. The divine vocation to humanity required a space of preparation for us to grow into it in its fullness: from the beginning, we were invited to embark on a journey of creaturely formation. We were created to change and be changed, to shape and be shaped – all in God's good time, because time is God's gift that enables us to grow towards the fullness of God's blessing. The sin of the first human beings was therefore essentially one of impatience: they snatched at the gift prematurely, rather than waiting for the giver to bestow it (cf. Phil. 2.6).

Yet while the consequences of sin are radical and profound, they do not end the story of God's call to human creatures and human responses to that; formation is always a possibility for human life so long as saying yes, at any level, to our creaturely vocation remains a possibility. While the shadows of sin – pain, domination, struggle and death – are at one level destructive, our creation in God's image, with our capacity for self-transcendence in knowledge, freedom and love, also renders them openings for our growth. In facing them, we can be changed in ways that correspond to our original calling from God to take responsibility for the earth and to love one another in shared endeavour and mutual delight. Pain elicits compassion, and compassion leads to action that brings relief and healing. Domination generates resistance and the striving for justice and for peace. The arduous struggle for survival becomes the catalyst for human work and the balancing activities of play as relief from labour, with the astounding diversity and creativity of both. All living things die, but human beings alone know that one day they will die, and in facing death, human beings can reach astonishing heights of goodness, courage and truth. The garden of Eden may have been wonderful, but we should also marvel at the achievements of agriculture, industry, science, technology and culture across the millennia. Even in alienation from God, the human race continues to respond, however crookedly, to the call of the creator. In pursuing what is good, not always with clear sight, it is always changing that with which it is confronted and itself changing as it does so in ways that fit – in part – the original purposes of goodness.

In my own experience of working with people studying theology and preparing for ministry, my impression is that facing these shadows of sin has often been a critical, difficult and powerfully productive moment in the formational journey. Pain, domination, struggle, death – they have the power to unbalance us, to shake us out of the complacency that so easily infects and paralyzes our lives, and to bring us to a sudden clearing where we become aware of new possibilities and choices. If the original sin in Genesis is an impatient grasping for the gift we should grow into in the course of creation's time, suffering, loss and mortality can starkly reveal to us our fundamental dependence and the limit of our restless efforts. Some of the darkest times in our lives can become the place from which we turn towards God and call on God with a depth and intensity of faith that we have not known before. Even there, we may be enabled to hear God's call to us and discern God's purpose for our days on earth with new clarity.

Chapter review

A reading of the opening chapters of Genesis shows how to be human is to be addressed by God and hence to be defined by divine vocation. From the beginning, humanity is called into a unique set of interwoven relationships, with the earth, with one another and with God. It is in the light of this whole picture that we can best understand the idea of human beings as made in the image of God. God gives humanity the space to exercise faith and to grow towards fullness of life, yet we have been unable to progress without failing in faith and falling into sin and a life marked by its shadows. God does not, however, cease to address us, and therefore in however flawed and halting a fashion, formation in response to our vocation as human persons also continues, even in the midst of pain, suffering and mortality.

5

Called through Christ

The Old Testament tells the story of how God continued to call out to humanity beyond the garden of Eden. The call is always new – addressed to new persons in new situations and transforming both – and always the same, in that it is a recalling of the purpose of creation. As in the beginning, it comes as promise and command, as invitation and judgement, and it asks to be received in faith, in reverence for the eternally faithful one, so that creation's motion towards its fulfilment can begin anew. The word of God's call comes with arresting directness to some, sometimes just one, and it seeks a home with them, through a relationship of mutual covenant between people and their God and the weaving of divine–human encounter into the rhythms of creaturely life. In the teaching of the commandments, in the word of the prophets and in the worship of the temple, Israel is formed for its vocation, which it is not given for its sake only but for the sake of the whole world. As God's servant, Israel is called to be a light for the nations. The horizon of God's purpose for all humanity and all creation is never lost. Still the word cannot find a settled home: as in the beginning, sin breaks up the movement of response and its shadows close around those who would shelter near to the place of the word's hearing. There is no straight path for living out the human vocation. Yet God keeps speaking. God keeps calling, and people do not cease to hear.

'And the Word became flesh and lived among us, and we have seen his glory, the glory as of a father's only son, full of grace and truth' (John 1.14). The Word that addressed humanity in the beginning, the Word that came to Israel and shone in and through it, the Word of God became flesh. The incarnation brings together God's call to humanity and humanity's response to that call. In Jesus, we see how God speaks to Israel and, through Israel, to the whole human race; we see how Israel and, through Israel, the whole human race might reply. In Jesus, then, we find both the outline of the vocation that comes to us from God and the pattern of the formation that enables us to say yes to this vocation. At the centre of a Christian theology of vocation and formation is Christ.

In order to consider what this might mean, we begin the chapter by looking at some themes in Jesus' calling of those he meets in the stories of the Gospels. We end the chapter by examining two titles of Jesus in the New Testament that help to illuminate further what it means to recognize in Jesus the self-communication of God and the origin and end of humanity: the Son of God, and the image of God. In the central section, I would like to ask, with some trepidation, the pivotal if theologically fraught question: what of the vocation and formation of Jesus himself? Is he shaped and changed as he responds to the Father's call? Only if the answer to that question is yes can he truly be the pioneer as well as the perfecter of our faith (Heb. 12.2), given that formation is an integral dimension of faith's journey as we experience it.

Jesus the bearer of God's call

From the beginning, at the heart of Jesus' call to others as recounted in the Gospels, is the proclamation of good news (Mark 1.14–15). The good news is not that something wholly without precedent is about to happen: rather, it is that God is faithful to the goodness of God's promises and that there is a new beginning, a new opening, for us to grow into the fullness of those promises. The fulfilment of what has been promised brings newness, because in such fulfilment there is always more than we could have asked or imagined on the basis of what we had known before. The call into God's promises, the call of God to Israel and the call of God in creation that stands behind it, therefore means renewal and transformation as well as restoration and confirmation. In Jesus' teaching, the symbol of this fullness through renewal and restoration is the kingdom, or reign, of God. The good news is that God's reign is near, at hand: we can seek it, welcome it, enter it.

It is a message Jesus brings to anyone who will listen, though how he communicates it varies. He may draw on parable, explanation, declaration, exclamation, lament or prophecy – often weaving together words and actions as he does so, as in what have been called the miracle stories. One remarkable constant, however, in his ministry of sharing this good news from God is that he calls people to respond to it first and foremost by being with him: by keeping company with him.

This seems to have been a feature of Jesus' ministry that perplexed even sympathetic observers, for at least two reasons. First, his initial communication by word or deed, even to notorious sinners, is that they are welcome to be with him. He does not say: repent, change your life and then I will sit down with you. Instead, the first thing he says to Zacchaeus, the hated and exploitative tax collector, is that he will come to his house and eat with him (Luke 19.1–10). Having been welcomed into his company, Zacchaeus recognizes how unjustly he has behaved in the past and that he needs to turn his life around and make reparation for the wrongs he has done. But Jesus does not make this a condition, nor is it recorded that he actually asked Zacchaeus to do it. Devout people might admire a teacher whose mission is 'to seek out and save the lost' (Luke 19.10), but this seemed like an eccentric if not dangerous way to go about it. This was particularly apparent when he was invited into their homes but then failed to turn away the sinners who followed him there (Luke 7.36–50).

Even Jesus' own disciples wondered at aspects of his behaviour relating to the sheer openness of the invitation to be in his company. A Jew, he lets himself be approached by Gentiles; a man in an intensely patriarchal society, he does not turn away the unaccompanied women who accost him – including those who are doubly unsuitable because of reputation or ethnicity or both; an adult under great pressures, he is happy to let his precious time be taken up by the idle business of embracing children. In all of these things, Jesus enacted a restoration of relationships that hinged on his welcoming presence.

Jesus' call to be in his company also worried and alienated some devout people because of the implication that somehow he was himself at the centre of the good news he went about proclaiming. Who was he that being with him and being near him should be so important? Why was the message inseparable from the one who proclaimed it? If he was truly passing on a call that came from God, why was it necessary that he should be there with us in order for us to receive it? He almost seemed to be saying that to enter the kingdom of God it was necessary to accept his authority; as if God's word to God's people was embodied in his person, and receiving that word meant receiving him, and ignoring him meant rejecting that word and heading again down the path of judgement; as if God's Word had become flesh.

For much of twentieth-century biblical studies, it was taken for granted that the idea of there being something special about who Jesus was (as opposed to what he said and did) only grew up after Jesus' death in the beliefs of the early Church. Some more recent scholars, however, have argued that it makes much better sense of the Gospels as historical documents to accept that in fact it begins with the first disciples and indeed with

Jesus himself.[31] Other teachers and leaders instinctively seemed to understand that Jesus of Galilee was making a powerful if for the most part implicit claim about himself and his relation to the fullness of God's purposes, and that this claim cut sharply across many of the things they took for granted about the ways of God in the world.

Jesus, then, proclaimed the good news of God's reign, in varied and creative ways, to the particular people he met around Galilee, Samaria and Judea, and he proclaimed it through his meeting with them. His words and actions interpreted the meaning of that specific meeting in relation to the call at the heart of it all to believe the good news: to receive this message and its messenger with faith, the recognition that here we are being addressed by the good and faithful God. The meaning of the meeting might be articulated in terms of repentance and forgiveness of sins, or healing, deliverance and restoration, or a specific call to leave behind work and home and family and follow Jesus in his itinerant ministry. It might also be articulated as judgement for resisting the good news and the one in whose person that good news becomes known, for the absence of faith; this is where the accent shifts as the action of the Gospels moves from Galilee to Jerusalem and towards the mystery of the rejection of God's anointed. The good news of God, the renewal of God's promises to Israel and through Israel for all creation, is not in the end received with joyful faith: we still do not believe. Even the faith of those who have been most in his company fails as he is taken to the cross. The Word which was from the beginning 'came to what was his own, and his own people did not accept him' (John 1.11).

At the centre of the earliest written Gospel is something that sounds like very bad news indeed: 'If any want to become my followers, let them deny themselves and take up their cross and

---

31 N. T. Wright, 1996, *Jesus and the Victory of God*, London: SPCK.

follow me' (Mark 8.34). This message brings us close to the heart of the New Testament as a whole. Jesus is speaking to the crowd and to his disciples at the pivotal point in the Gospel narrative when Peter has gloriously discerned his identity as God's anointed and then been utterly dismayed at his prophecies of rejection and suffering. To receive the good news from Jesus, we have to be prepared to share also in his suffering and rejection. We need to let go of the life we have lived, of the self into which we have grown that is shot through with suspicion and resistance in the face of God's goodness. We will have to find the courage and determination to keep following Jesus when the way of discipleship leads to us losing affection, respect and security. In the end, to receive the Word made flesh we have to let die everything that holds us back from believing the good news and entering the kingdom in the company of Jesus: our sins, yes, but also our sinful attachments, not just to unjustly gained wealth but even to what is most properly and closely ours, because those attachments have shaped our inmost selves for destruction and not for life (Mark 9.43–48). To enter the reign of God we will have to begin again from the depths of our personhood and be born anew from God, in order to become children of God (John 3.1–15).

We receive God's call, then, from Christ and with Christ, in his company. The message he brings is inseparable from the person he is. Listening to God's word means drawing near to the Word become flesh: because of the incarnation, we find our vocation in Christ and never apart from Christ. Christian formation is therefore always about being changed by, in and for the presence of Christ. In that presence, we hear God's call as good news: news of restoration and renewal, confirmation of God's faithfulness and transformation of all that blocks the fullness of God's will, for with Christ we can begin to enter God's reign. The necessary transformation, however, has to include confrontation with the tenacity of evil in ourselves and in our world: the joyful news of God's grace also discloses the tragic extent of the ways in which we are bound by sin to the power of sin and held back from dwelling in God's reign. In order to receive all that is offered to us by God in the person of Jesus, we have to let go of the self we have become without him. Nor is this something that we simply do once and for all: it is a constant dimension of the formational journey, and one that constantly clears new ground for receiving as whole persons from the person of Christ the good news of God's invitation. There is no following Jesus without carrying the cross.

Jesus the hearer of God's call

In Jesus, the Word becomes flesh, a human being. Jesus is therefore both the one who bears God's call to others with unique power and the one who hears God's call to himself with unique clarity. It is because he bears it that he hears it so intensely and because he hears it that he bears it so truthfully.

Where we begin to tread on more delicate theological territory is with the question of whether for Jesus as for us, hearing the call of God means being shaped and therefore changed in responding to that call. Much traditional Christology has been acutely uncomfortable with the idea that Jesus changes in any way that relates to his mind rather than 'merely' his body (as if the two were independent): his free acceptance of God's will, his knowledge and understanding, his love of God and of human beings. While there have been some genuine theological reasons for this discomfort, it is a presumption that must be questioned and should be rejected.[32] First, as I hope to sketch out in a moment, it does not correspond with the scriptural

---

32 Alan Spence, 1991, 'Christ's Humanity and Ours: John Owen', in Christoph Schwöbel and Colin E. Gunton (eds), *Persons, Divine and Human: King's College Essays in Theological Anthropology*, Edinburgh: T. & T. Clark, pp. 74–97.

witness. Second, it leaves us with no coherent account of Jesus' humanity, since we know that change through learning, experiment and response is integral to human life. Third, it would mean that Christians in formation cannot look to Christ as example or companion. It would mean that Jesus did not have any share in the formational journey of human creatures, and that cannot be the truth if the Word truly became flesh and dwelt among us.

Jesus grows in wisdom as he grows also in years, according to Luke 2.52. This comment occurs at the end of Luke's account of a family visit to the Jerusalem temple when Jesus is twelve years old. During the visit, they lose him because he stays in the temple after everyone else from the party has left, 'sitting among the teachers, listening to them and asking them questions' (Luke 2.46). He is already full of wisdom (Luke 2.40), a wisdom that astounds those who hear him (Luke 2.47). Yet it is part of being wise that one should share one's understanding with others in the right circumstances and that one is prepared to receive understanding from others in turn and from the unpredictable conversation that ensues. That is how human beings grow in wisdom: through the exchange of understanding and the creative encounter that then unfolds around it.

Does Jesus continue to grow in understanding as his ministry finally unfolds? There is not much in the Gospels that obviously helps us to explore this. Some commentators would interpret the story of Jesus' encounter with the Syrophoenician woman in these terms (Mark 7.24–30 and parallels). Initially, Jesus appears to brush off her request for him to cast out a demon from her daughter, on the grounds that his vocation is only to Israel (as Matthew makes explicit in his version, at Matt. 15.24). Yet her response of faith to his person – conveyed through a wise and witty rejoinder – leads to a change of mind. He heals her daughter. Through the encounter, through the robust exchange of perspectives and concerns, his perception of his own vocation has shifted. He has a different understanding, and it leaves him free to act in a way that he had not been before. It leaves him free to express the love of God in loving action in a way that he had not been before.

The writers of the Synoptic Gospels are more interested, however, in how Jesus holds together the knowledge of being chosen to bear God's call with facing what in the previous chapter we called the shadows of sin: pain, domination, struggle and death. That Jesus learns and indeed is made perfect through this is also clearly a theme of great significance for the writer of the letter to the Hebrews (Heb. 2.10–18; 5.7–10). For the word to become flesh means that God's call becomes implicated in the fractured dynamics of human living that have always up to this point prevented the fully faithful hearing of the word. Will the story be repeated with Jesus? Will the shadows keep overwhelming the light?

This is the critical issue for the accounts of Jesus' temptation in the wilderness (Mark 1.12–13; Matt. 4.1–11; Luke 4.1–13). It is no accident that these are placed immediately after his baptism by John. As he emerges from the water, Jesus is called by God: he is named as God's son, God's beloved. We may assume, I think, that this is both the affirmation of a truth Jesus has long known and also a new and arresting experience; hence the need for time and space to figure out what it means and how he is to respond. We have a model here for the way that any significant new step in understanding our vocation needs a fresh space for formation as we prepare to move into it.

Matthew and Luke dramatize Jesus' struggle to discern where his vocation as God's son may be taking him in terms of a series of three exchanges between Jesus and the devil, the tempter. As in the garden of Eden, to come near to the fullness of God's gift is to draw out the presence of evil and be tested by it. The word of the tempter is essentially the same as it was to Adam and Eve: can you really put your faith in God? Can you really be sure of

God's goodness, God's faithfulness? Would it not be better to try a few moves to make God confirm what he has said, so you can put to one side your suspicions? By contrast with the garden of Eden, however, Jesus remains faithful in the face of such testing. He continues to say yes with his whole being to the call of God – to be who he is as God's son.

These few short verses deserve lengthy interpretation, but let me just highlight one way that we might approach them. We can read the three temptations as invitations to Jesus to use his unique vocation to continue the distortion of human relations that has followed from human sinfulness – to deepen the shadows of sin. Following Luke's order, the first of Jesus' temptations in the wilderness is to see in this vocation the opportunity to satisfy his own hunger. Satan suggests to Jesus that God's gift of power to rule over the earth, which he now holds anew, could be used to meet his needs and desires. His response shows us the meaning of the command in the beginning to have dominion: it is not an invitation to do what we want with the earth and treat it as a collection of 'resources' for our own satisfaction, but as the place where we learn what it means to live at God's hand. Later in the Gospels, Jesus is represented as one whose authority indeed extends to the non-human creation. In the midst of a life-threatening storm, he speaks to the wind and the waves – and they obey. He curses a fig tree – and it withers. He takes a handful of loaves and fishes and gives thanks to the one who created them – and they become abundant enough to feed thousands. People eat bread joyfully in his company – but not 'by the sweat of your face' (Gen. 3.19). Yet such authority is only claimed for the sake of his specific vocation to bear the message of good news and call people to enter God's reign.

The second temptation is to find in the unique vocation of being God's son a licence for the domination of all other people: 'To you I will give their glory and all this authority' (Luke 4.6). Why not, if he is so special, indeed unique, in the eyes of God? Jesus immediately perceives, however, that the price of worship from other people is the transfer of our own worship to the power of our destruction; those who dominate others become themselves dominated by darkness. Freedom for human beings is in worshipping and serving God alone and not seeking to be a divine object for humankind. The third temptation is to call into question God's will for our good by deliberately engaging in self-destructive behaviour so that God will ride to the rescue. It is to agree that faith cannot be simple and whole-hearted but must be mingled with suspicion if it is to be really mature. It is to seek to manipulate God into doing something that puts him within our powers, that can bind him to us, as if only idolatry were truly worship. The resistance to these temptations also sets the pattern for how Jesus will practise relationship to other people and to God in his ministry. He will seek to set free and not to subjugate, to celebrate the reality of God's goodness here and now and not to contrive spectacles of religious power to generate shock and awe.

At the heart of Jesus' formation, then, is a testing and a wrestling that relates at once to the utterly particular context arising from his baptism and to the proper relation for all humanity with the earth, with one another and with God. It is vital that we see how these two things are inseparable here, for the same will also apply to us. To go forward in our response to God's call will always be about specific choices that face us in the light of our contingent and unique circumstances, and also about how we will live out our common vocation as human creatures to sustain right relationships with the world, the people around us and the God who calls us. There will always be a temptation to think that the particularity of my vocation here and now somehow makes me special in a way that exempts me from growing into the 'ordinary' human vocation to right relationships. The more strongly we feel ourselves called to some distinctive form of ministerial responsibility or spiritual life, the more powerful this temptation may well become.

Luke ends his account of the temptations in the wilderness by noting that the devil 'departed from him until an opportune time' (Luke 4.13). That time, we may infer, is when Jesus faces finally and fully the suffering into which faithfulness to his vocation is leading him, in the garden of Gethsemane (Luke 22.39–46). Why should he, the Son of God, be handed over to the power of others, when he could take power over them? Would not that be a better way to fulfil his calling, would not that be more pleasing to the Father? And why should he, the Son of God, suffer judgement, mockery and humiliation from those who believe they are God's chosen? Would it not be far better to call on God to vindicate him through a miraculous deliverance, so that all Jerusalem might know who he really is? What is to be gained by dying, when the word of God is life? As he grapples with these questions in prayer for the last and decisive time, 'his sweat became like great drops of blood falling down on the ground' (Luke 22.44). This too is formation, formation in faith. Faith in God does not mean that the way is always clear or that we never need to question God. At one point the Bible traces the roots of the word 'Israel' as meaning 'the one who strives with God' (cf. Gen. 32.28), and here in Gethsemane Jesus shares in the formation of Israel through the struggle with Israel's God. In his agony over what on earth the good God he has been proclaiming can intend by the ending of his life in utter humiliation and excruciating pain, Jesus indeed becomes 'the pioneer and perfecter of our faith' (Heb. 12.2), our example and our companion on the way of formation.

God the only Son

It is in the prologue to John's Gospel that we find the claim that Jesus is God's eternal Word become flesh, the Word that was with God from the beginning, the Word that was God (John

1.1–18). The prologue also interweaves 'Word' with other terms to express the identity of Jesus. One of these is 'son': 1.14 speaks of the glory of the Word 'as of a father's only son'. The implication seems to be that the sharing of the Word in God's reality might be compared to the way a father confers all that he has on an only son. The final, climactic verse of the prologue moves beyond this incidental reference to leave 'Son' as the final key to knowing who we are really meeting in Jesus of Nazareth. 'No one has ever seen God. It is God the only Son, who is close to the Father's heart, who has made him known' (John 1.18).

'Son', like 'Word', implies communication in this context: the Son is the one who by acting on the Father's behalf enables the Father to be known. The Son speaks the Father's words; the Father's call is transmitted through the Son. Yet 'Son' implies something more, and it is no accident that this becomes the critical term for John's Gospel and for the Johannine literature as a whole. To begin with, the relationship of Son to Father is not only communicative. It is not only an outward relationship of making known, it is also an inward relationship of love, of being known. The Father wants to be with the Son because he is the Father and this is his Son, and not only because the Father wishes to say or do something further. And the Son is a person: a divine person. The Word that becomes flesh is not an abstraction, an emanation, an idea or an agency. It is not something, but someone: the Son of God. No other word can convey all this, which is why although I appreciate and share the concern to balance the dominance of male-gendered terms in traditional theology by using alternative expressions, the understanding of Jesus as God's Son must remain pivotal for the theology of Christian vocation.

The prologue of John's Gospel makes some paradoxical assertions about divinity: the Word is with God and also is God; the God whom no one has ever seen is made known by God the only Son. In the so-called 'Farewell Discourses' (John 14—17),

the Gospel provides an extended meditation on the dynamics of divine and human relationships as they are revealed in
Christ. How can someone be both identified with another and
yet also in relation to that other? Jesus asserts repeatedly, for
instance, that 'I am in the Father and the Father is in me' (e.g.
John 14.11), yet he also says very clearly that he is 'going to the
Father' (e.g. John 14.12). He is present there already, and yet
there is distance to be traversed. He is one with the Father, yet
still he says 'you' to this Father and is addressed by him and
responds to him. We are being shown that there is a relation of
call and response within the Godhead itself: the Word was with
God in the beginning, and the Word was God.

These passages had a vital role in shaping what came to be
articulated as the doctrine of the Trinity in the fourth century.
The beloved Son cannot be separated from the eternal Father:
the two are, in the terminology that was later developed, of one
substance, one 'being'. Yet the Son addresses the Father and
the Father addresses the Son in a relationship of love, which
always also implies plurality and distinction: therefore they are,
again in the terminology developed in the fourth century, two
persons or 'hypostases'. At the same time, it was discerned that
the Holy Spirit likewise cannot be distinguished from God and
yet is likewise in a relation of love to the Father and the Son. In
other words, for the God in whose image we were created it is
the case that being and relationship are inseparable: for God's
being is communion. God is communion in eternity and in
Godself, because God is love in eternity and in Godself, a line of
thought developed by Richard of St Victor in the twelfth century.[33] The concept of 'person' as we know it today (and indeed
have been using it in this book in relation to human beings)

---

33 Richard of St Victor, 1979, *The Twelve Patriarchs, The Mystical Ark,
Book Three of the Trinity*, trans. Grover A. Zinn, Mahwah, New Jersey: Paulist
Press, pp. 371–97.

emerges from this rich vein of theological thought that originates in the early centuries of the Church, and there has to be a
question as to whether an appreciation of the reality of human
personhood can survive uprooting from it.[34]

It is no accident that the section of the New Testament that
was among the most important for developing Trinitarian doctrine is also among the richest for reflecting on what it means
for humanity to be called into communion with God through
Christ. Towards the end of the Farewell Discourses, Jesus prays
to the Father: 'As you, Father, are in me and I am in you, may
they also be in us, so that the word may believe that you have
sent me' (John 17.21b). As in Christ we meet the beloved Son
of God, so to be in Christ is to share in the eternal life of God
which embraces the love that flows between Father, Son and
Spirit. It is to find 'my' self with human others within God's
Trinitarian being. It is to know a unity with human others and
with God that does not efface my unique 'I' any more than the
unity of Father, Son and Holy Spirit effaces their distinction.
God is revealed through Christ as love from all eternity, and
there is no love without 'I' and 'you' in abiding communion.

The image of the invisible God

The letter to the Colossians includes a passage that links together
the naming of Christ as God's Son with another scriptural concept: the image of God, to which we gave some attention in
the previous chapter. The poetic character of the verses has led
some scholars to argue that they might be a quotation from an
early Christian hymn familiar to the writer and his audience:

---

34 John D. Zizioulas, 1997, *Being as Communion: Studies in Personhood
and the Church*, Crestwood, New York: St Vladimir's Seminary Press; Robert
Spaemann, 2006, *Persons: The Difference between 'Someone' and 'Something'*,
ET, Oxford: Oxford University Press.

He is the image of the invisible God, the firstborn of all creation; for in him all things in heaven and on earth were created, things visible and invisible, whether thrones or dominions or rulers or powers – all things have been created through him and for him. He himself is before all things, and in him all things hold together. (Col. 1.15–17)

The claim that is being made here has profound implications for how we read the witness of the Scriptures as a whole. To begin with what might seem too obvious to labour: the Son *is* the image of God, an assertion we also find at 2 Cor. 4.4.[35] In Genesis 1, humanity is made *in* the image of God, but Jesus, the Son of God, is now revealed as this image in which we are all made. He is the model, the original for humanity, beginning with Adam and Eve, and because of the primacy of humanity, 'the firstborn of all creation'. The ground of humanity's creation is thereby located within the divine life itself.

A further point follows on from this. The end of humanity that is revealed in Christ is what God 'meant' in creating humanity in the beginning. God's purpose from the beginning was that the Son through whom all things were created should be the one through whom all creation responds to God in the end – led by humanity. The incarnation of the Word in Jesus is a new thing that God does in time. The purpose that thereby comes to fulfilment, however, is not new at all but reaches back to the act of creation. It is in the beloved Son, who is God's own image, that human beings become what God has always wanted them to be. This point is crucial not least in resisting the tendency of Western theology since the Middle Ages to shrink the

---

35 On the importance of the image of God for the theology of the New Testament as a whole, see Stanley J. Grenz, 2001, *The Social God and the Relational Self: A Trinitarian Theology of the* Imago Dei, Louisville, Kentucky: Westminster John Knox, pp. 203–22.

doctrine of salvation to 'the question of how God forgives sins, and, specifically, whether he has forgiven mine'.[36]

Does this mean that the incarnation itself is intrinsic to God's purposes in creation, rather than a response to human sin only? That was the conclusion reached by a number of important figures from different traditions of medieval theology, including Maximus the Confessor, and John Duns Scotus. Although it had not been widely affirmed in the West, over the past hundred years a clear consensus has emerged among major theologians that Christian doctrine cannot understand God's creation of the world and of human beings within it in isolation from the event of the Word becoming flesh in Jesus and dwelling among us. Humanity was created to become the dwelling place of God through God's self-communication in free self-gift. The theology of creation and the theology of the incarnation are properly interwoven in Christian understanding:

> The world came into being, it was created and sustained by the little child that was born in Bethlehem, by the man who died on the Cross of Golgotha, and the third day rose again. *That* is the Word of creation, by which all things were brought into being.[37]

The quotation is from Karl Barth, but without denying significant differences we can identify the same insistence on holding together creation and incarnation in twentieth-century Roman Catholic theology, as well as in contemporary Orthodox writing.[38]

---

36 Ellen T. Charry, 1997, *By the Renewing of Your Minds: The Pastoral Function of Christian Doctrine*, Oxford: Oxford University Press, p. 128.

37 Karl Barth, 1949, *Dogmatics in Outline*, ET London: SCM, p. 58.

38 Robert Kress, 1986, 'The Catholic Understanding of Human Nature', in Frederick E. Greenspahn (ed.), *The Human Condition in the Jewish and Christian Traditions*, Hoboken, New Jersey: Ktav, pp. 26–72; Olivier Clément, 2000, *On Human Being: A Spiritual Anthropology*, London: New City, pp. 25–42.

The point may seem rather technical, but it is profoundly important for the way that we think about Christian vocation and hence about Christian formation. We do not exist first as independent creatures – or autonomous selves – and only then enter into a relationship to Christ. Along with all creation, we are created 'through him and for him'. To become who we are, therefore, we must follow in the footsteps of Jesus; and through faithful discipleship of Christ, we will begin to shine with the radiance for which we were created. We are summoned by the one who is the original image for our being, and responding to that call is therefore the only true path to human fulfilment. There is no fulfilment, however, for the 'self' that we seek to establish as separate from God's Word, God's Wisdom, God's Son, because such a self denies the truth. Only through denial of that denial can the human person in the end find the way to life. There is ultimately no way of meeting the needs and expectations that arise from imagining ourselves as separate from who we are in Christ – through Christian discipleship and ministry or indeed through their rejection. As Christian theology cannot make sense of creation without reference to the incarnation, so we cannot make sense of ourselves outside of the mystery of our salvation. Our deep-seated resistance here is not simply a matter of psychological or cultural conditioning, but about sin and the way it invites us to wall ourselves off from the reality of God's grace, to live without faith.

To affirm the incarnation as the key to creation also helps us to understand that our calling in Christ does not begin with our conscious exposure to Christian culture, nor rely on our sustained assent to its messages. If the Son of God is the image in whom we are made, then to be human is in itself to be always in some kind of relationship to the one who becomes incarnate in Christ: it is to be addressed by the eternal Word. If there is no point in our lives when we are not being addressed by God's Word, there is no point either where some kind of response to this Word is not a possibility for us, and therefore no point where we may not be shaped by that response. Christian formation then is not only about times when we are especially aware of hearing God's call in Christ, or indeed only about our deliberate efforts to respond to it. What may be happening at such times takes place within a longer and deeper history of our formation, which begins before we can name God and may continue when we think ourselves estranged from God. Indeed, while the Church is the context for our intentional response to God's call through Christ (the subject of the next chapter), we should not presume that it is the only place where the Word is being heard or attended to. The Word who became flesh does not cease to call out to all creation.

Chapter review

Jesus proclaims the good news through his presence, calling people into a relationship of abundant life. He also, however, teaches his shocked disciples that for them as for him, faithfulness to God's call leads towards death, and only through death to resurrection. As the pioneer and perfecter of our faith he too is shaped by God's call, and we catch glimpses of this in the Gospels. Jesus' truly human formation is both pattern and encouragement for us. In his risen humanity he is recognized as the eternal Son of God who calls us into communion with God, and as the divine image in which we are created. Our human personhood in time is inseparable from the communion of divine persons in eternity.

6

Responding as the Church

The purpose of God's call

> We know that all things work together for good for those who
> love God, who are called according to his purpose. For those
> whom he foreknew he also predestined to be conformed to
> the image of his Son, in order that he might be the firstborn
> within a large family. And those whom he predestined he also
> called; and those whom he called he also justified; and those
> whom he justified he also glorified. (Rom. 8.28–30)

This familiar passage brings together many of the threads we
have been following in the previous two chapters. It speaks of
those who respond to the love of the creator being 'called according to his purpose' and then sketches out with great brevity the
breadth and the depth of what that purpose might be. At the centre of it are the words: 'conformed to the image of his Son'. It is
in the light of this understanding of the purpose of God's calling,
received through Christ, that we now interpret the many and various ways in which God has spoken in the past (Heb. 1.1–2) and
direct our different responses in the present. There is no response
to God's call to us in Christ, and therefore no aspect of Christian
vocation, that is not oriented towards this one point. It is therefore here that we need to begin our exploration in this chapter
of how we respond as the Church to the call of God in Christ.

It is a purpose that brings together three of the major themes to emerge in the previous chapter. To be conformed to the image of God's Son is to be conformed to the image of the unseen God according to which humankind was created. Such conformity must include the restoration of this image and likeness within us, so that we can begin to live on earth in a way that expresses the overflowing goodness and generosity of the creator. In finding right relation with God in faith, we can also begin to dwell in right relation with one another and with the whole earth. Jesus shows us through his life that this can be a reality even in the midst of sin and its continuing shadows. He calls men and women into his company so that they can share the renewal of creation's purposes. No wonder, as Paul wrote a little earlier in Romans, that 'the creation waits with eager longing for the revealing of the children of God' (Rom. 8.19).

In the renewal of God's promise in creation, we also begin to see a depth of glory that we had not imagined before. God's purpose is for us to be conformed to the Son, the one who has been with the Father from the beginning and from all eternity. It is to be called into the divine communion of the Trinity that has no beginning and no end. The will of the creator is that creatures should share in the very life from which creation itself comes. Paul presses here at the limits of human thinking in response to the Word made flesh in Christ, but he is pressed to say that this purpose does not occur after our creation, as if God only then saw a possibility that had previously escaped divine thought. Rather, the purpose of eternal conformity to the image of the eternal Son is the reason, the ground, the origin of our being in time. Only in the light of God's purpose, now revealed in Christ, can we begin to grasp the unfathomable truth of who we are.

In order that we should begin to know and live these truths, the Son from eternity became a human being in time, Jesus of Nazareth. The call to be conformed to the image of the eternal Son is inseparable from the call to follow Jesus: we can only grasp them together, as illuminating and interpreting each other. Hence conformity to the image of God's Son means keeping company with Jesus today, in Galilee and in Jerusalem, in joyful witness to the reign of God and in painful relinquishment of the deep roots of our selfhood in sin and death, in celebration of God's abundance and in confrontation with the powers of darkness that bind men and women to evil. And as in the Gospels so today, there is no keeping company with Jesus without also keeping the company he keeps, and it is unlikely to be entirely the same people whom we would have chosen.

The purpose of our calling, then, is becoming conformed to the image of the Son, and we can identify three inseparable aspects of that: renewal of the image in which we were created, participation in God's eternal life and following Jesus day by day. The purpose is for me and I must respond from myself, from the core of my own being. Yet it is also true that I can only respond with others and that our response must itself contain the desire that together with all humanity we may grow into the fullness of this purpose: 'in order that he might be the firstborn within a large family'. My response to God's call is only found in our response: renewed relationships with other human persons, communion together with the triune God and the shared journey of discipleship. That common response is the Church. And as in the Church I cannot seek this purpose for myself without also seeking it for you, so the Church cannot seek it for itself without also seeking it for the whole world. There is no renewal of the image or participation in God's life or discipleship of Jesus which is content with the restriction of these gifts to some people only. If this is the purpose of God's call, then our response has to have each of these dimensions: from myself, with others and also for others, always desiring to grow together into the fullness of God's gift.

Shared response: the sacraments of the Church

Back at the start of Part 1, I tried to stress that secular formation happens primarily through our participation in shared practices that communicate narratives of human fulfilment. In the chapters that followed, we reflected on family life, economic activity and cultural pursuits – among other things – as examples of this, carrying more or less overt messages about fulfilment through freedom, knowledge and love. As we turn our attention more directly to Christian formation, it is important to bear in mind that we are still talking about human beings, and that shared practices and the messages they embody still have the primary place. It is the articulation of the Church's response to God's call through its distinctive practices that creates the basic 'texture' of Christian formation.[39]

Among the rich diversity of those practices, baptism and Eucharist have a special, central place. Traditionally, they have been distinguished from other things that Christians do by being called sacraments; while Catholic traditions may also refer to other practices as sacraments, there is an ecumenical consensus that these two have a particular primacy as acts by which the Church is defined. This is not to deny the value of forms of worship, service and discipleship that may seem to happen 'outside' of them, though I would want to argue that everything that the Church does always in fact stands in some kind of relation to baptism and Eucharist as Church-constituting events, flowing into them or out of them or indeed representing parts of them that have for one reason or another become detached. Sacraments are things that the Church does in faithfulness to God's Word to us in Christ which tell us and tell the world about the mystery of that Word made flesh, and also occasions where God has promised to be present in action that draws us

---

39 Andrew Davison and Alison Milbank, 2010, *For the Parish: A Critique of Fresh Expressions*, London: SCM, pp. 10–15.

into that mystery here and now; 'signs' but also 'instruments', in one piece of traditional terminology. They therefore have a primary place in giving shape to the life of the Church as the shared response of humanity to God's call through Christ.

While we rightly talk about the two sacraments of baptism and Eucharist, it is also the case that we cannot understand either sacrament in isolation from the other. To be baptized is to become part of the body of Christ: part of the eucharistic fellowship that lives by the bread of life broken in its midst. To share in the Eucharist is to join the thankful gathering of those who have been baptized: it is here that we discover what our baptism really means. Baptism enacts the response to God's call in Christ from each unique person as the desire to join the body of Christ in mission to the world; the Eucharist enacts the renewal of the shared response of that body in its movement from gathering to word and from meal to dismissal.

What, then, is the narrative of human fulfilment that we learn by participating in these cardinal practices of the Church? That is not a simple question to answer. Scholars have come to stress the plurality of overlapping theological themes and narratives within each sacrament, which cannot and should not be reduced to a single, fundamental 'meaning'.[40] Moreover, the actual narratives communicated in a given context to particular people, while bearing some relationship to these themes and narratives, will inevitably be coloured by the distinctive culture and circumstances of the worshipping community where the sacrament is being celebrated. The combination of word and action in both cases, however, draws us into an overarching narrative of fulfilment that can only appear deeply paradoxical: resurrection from the dead.

---

40 World Council of Churches, 1982, *Baptism, Eucharist and Ministry*, Faith and Order Paper 111, Geneva: World Council of Churches.

Do you not know that all of us who have been baptized into Christ Jesus were baptized into his death? Therefore we have been buried with him by baptism into death, so that, just as Christ was raised from the dead by the glory of the Father, so we too might walk in newness of life. (Rom. 6.3–4)

The paradox here is that death means the end of the story, and therefore the failure of fulfilment. Yet this end which is really an end becomes an opening, and this failure which really is the failing of the self we have made is the recovery of the person God created us to be. The purpose of our calling, being conformed to the image of God's Son, can only be fulfilled through resurrection from the dead in union with Christ, and that means being conformed to the cross. The sign of the cross in baptism and at other moments in the Christian life marks us out as those who have this hope: 'That I may know him, and the power of his resurrection, and the fellowship of his sufferings, being made conformable unto his death' (Phil. 3.10 [AV]). This is the mystery enacted in baptism, renewed in the Eucharist and communicated in every action of the Church that expresses its being.

Perhaps the sharpest formulation of this paradoxical gospel of human fulfilment occurs in Galatians 2.19–20:

For through the law I died to the law, so that I might live to God. I have been crucified with Christ; and it is no longer I who live, but it is Christ who lives in me. And the life I now live in the flesh I live by faith in the Son of God, who loved me and gave himself for me.

'I' died, yet 'I' live; the same 'I'? Surely not: 'it is no longer I who live, but Christ who lives in me'. Lives in whom, however? And how can Paul immediately proceed to say, 'the life I now live'? And who is the 'me' whom the Son of God loved, if not this same 'I', Paul, who both died and yet lives, in whom Christ lives and who lives by faith in Christ? The language of resurrection conveys both the continuity of personhood between the one who died and the one who is raised (for it is truly *we* who are raised) and the radical discontinuity of selfhood between these two (for we truly *died*, our lives were finished). Resurrection is not a pious word for personal survival, but the unthinkable claim that death which overcomes all life has itself been overcome. That claim becomes thinkable not because of some argument or concept, but because of Jesus, whom we encounter as risen and can now for the first time recognize as the one through whom and for whom we were created in the beginning and who has overcome everything that distorts and destroys our humanity. 'For you have died, and your life is hidden with Christ in God. When Christ who is your life is revealed, then you also will be revealed with him in glory' (Col. 3.3–4). This risen life is with us now but is also still to come, both present and absent here on earth. That too belongs to the narrative of human fulfilment that is carried by the Church's practices.

In the early centuries of Christianity, it was normal for baptism to lead straight into a special celebration of the Eucharist and then into regular participation in the weekly Eucharist from that point onwards. What do we do, what do we say, as those who have lost their old lives and been raised to new life in baptism, though new life which still remains 'hidden'? First, we come together with those who have also been baptized. We assemble. This is what it means to be the Church: the Greek term we translate as 'Church', *ekklesia*, has 'assembly' as its basic meaning. And we assemble as the Church by God's grace 'in order that you may proclaim the mighty acts of him who called you out of darkness into his marvellous light' (1 Peter 2.9): our gathering as witnesses to the resurrection has to overflow first and foremost in thanksgiving, worship and praise. Second, we turn to the Scriptures of Israel and the Church and we hear preaching and teaching arising from our reading of them. Third, we share a meal in which we remember the presence of the crucified and risen Son of God who broke bread with his disciples on the night before he died, in whom we have communion with God and with one another and with the Church in every place. Fourth, we seek the fulfilment of that purpose according to which we were called through intercession, through practical service (including gifts for the poor) and through being sent out to live our daily lives in the name of Jesus Christ, for the gifts we celebrate in our gathering cannot be confined to it.

One name for the weekly gathering that brought these four elements together from at least the second century is the Eucharist (which means 'thanksgiving'). Whether or not we follow a similar pattern in our church today, these four areas of activity are fundamental to the pattern of the Church's response to God's call through Jesus Christ. Moreover, it is clearly important that they do not become detached from one another: worship needs to be anchored in reading the Scriptures together, just as study of the Scriptures needs to flow into both praise and prayer; sharing the Communion meal needs to both illuminate and be illuminated by scriptural teaching, just as it needs to be a meeting with the one who loves the world with all its tragedies, needs and sins and who calls us also to meet him there.[41]

The four elements I have identified – assembling for praise, attending to the Scriptures, sharing bread and wine in memory of Christ and acting in prayer, witness and service in Christ's name – are held together within the Eucharist itself by the third, the sharing of bread and wine. They find their meaning and their home in relation to this. But that is not to say that they do not happen at any other time. From a very early stage, some

---

41 My thinking here is influenced by, though it does not exactly follow, Gordon W. Lathrop, 1993, *Holy Things: A Liturgical Theology*, Minneapolis, Minnesota: Fortress.

kind of daily participation in praise and intercession has been expected of Christians as integral to sharing in the Church's response to God's call in Christ; attending to the Scriptures through hearing them in the Sunday assembly has also frequently been extended beyond it either by individual reading, meeting in smaller groups or listening to teaching in other contexts. We will take a closer look at this in the next chapter.

More than this, however, the reason why the dismissal is such an essential part of the eucharistic liturgy is that it denies that this liturgy is a self-contained action: instead, what happens in the Eucharist is always passing over into what exists outside it (at one level) in order to transform it so that it too can be gathered into the symphony of creation's praise. We will not begin to understand the Eucharist if we think that our participation in its reality stops once we return to 'ordinary' life. We are the body of Christ here also, responding to the call of God here also, guided in all our activity by the glorious purpose of becoming conformed to the image of the Son here also. Christian vocation is about the whole of our lives. Its beginning may be in baptism and its heartbeat in the Eucharist, but its articulation is in our days, our weeks and our years. God does not cease to address us when we walk out of church, close our Bibles or get up from prayer, or to invite us to answer that address. There is no situation that cannot become an occasion for God to speak to us or to speak through us to others, and correspondingly no situation where we cannot welcome or indeed refuse God's Word.

The sacraments of baptism and Eucharist shape our shared response as Church to God's call through Christ. There is nothing we do in response to that call that does not somehow fit into this rhythm – that does not flow from our baptism and flow back into the Eucharist, to be offered up in praise or intercession and brought with us as we gather around the Lord's table week by week. There is also therefore nothing that happens in our formation for vocation that does not also belong within the same underlying rhythm that is set by the Church's sacraments. This conclusion reflects a widespread movement within recent theological writing which strongly affirms the life of the Church as the context for learning what it means to follow the call of Christ and the distinctive practices of the Church as integral to Christian formation.[42]

In the next two sections of the chapter, I want to move on to consider contexts where we are likely to be more familiar with the language of vocation, in the sense of particular ways of responding to God's call that are common to some but not all – the 'distinctive vocations' that I mentioned at the end of the Preface. Before doing that, however, I would stress the importance of keeping in mind that these things too are part of our shared response as the Church, that they flow from our baptism and flow back into our participation in the Eucharist. They come from us, yes, but this is inseparable from their being undertaken *with* others who are also responding and *for* others so that they may respond more fully. Understanding this can help us to overcome the impasse of individual versus institutional approaches to vocation that we have touched on a couple of times already: 'my' vocation is never just about me, but a dimension of my participation in the common vocation of the whole Church, constituted by baptism and Eucharist, to bring good news to the whole world.

Distinctive vocations: vocations of daily life

I know the fervour with which students looking forward to ordination sing words taken from the biblical story of Samuel: 'Here I am, Lord.' It is relatively easy to get excited about vocation

---

42 See for example Samuel Wells, 2006, *God's Companions: Reimagining Christian Ethics*, Malden, Massachusetts: Blackwell.

when it involves taking up a special place, a place of public recognition, within the Church. But Christian vocation is a daily response to the call of God to go out into the world in company with Christ as witnesses to Christ.

The way that we do this will be configured in very significant ways by the pattern of our work and the pattern of our relationships. At various times, it is likely to be the case that we have no great control over these things: we are all born into a network of relationships in our family of origin that is set prior to our arrival, even if we begin to influence it as soon as we are there; during years of compulsory education, our work is more or less prescribed by the state and the institutions where we study; illness, old age and poverty are likely to diminish our scope for making choices in such matters at some points in our adult lives. Yet most of us will also make critical decisions, more or less consciously and reflectively, about the kind of work we do and the kind of household relationships we have. While this may not seem like a natural way of speaking, I would like to suggest that we may helpfully see such decisions in terms of distinctive vocations of daily life: commitments that shape in critical ways the context for how we will participate in the shared response of the Church to the call of God in Christ, opening up one set of possibilities and closing down others.

For most of us, the majority of our waking hours are given over to work, in one form or another. Can this really be part of our Christian vocation? Our work has a critical role in drawing us into the web of practices that drive our secular formation, as discussed in Part 1 of this book. We then saw in Chapter 4 how Genesis imagines work in the beginning as a response to the call of God to take responsibility for nurturing the earth and for bringing order that both sustains what God has made and called good and creates new patterns and possibilities through our interaction with it. Yet Genesis also sees the effects of alienation from God in the way that work is so often hard and exhausting, depriving us of energy and deadening our ability to delight in the world that God has made. Work can draw us into pain, domination and struggle – those shadows of sin from which it can be difficult to see the light of God. For those called to follow Christ, it should become a place where we face those shadows but are not overcome by them, to share in the renewal of creation and to begin to live the fullness of what it means to be in Christ and therefore in the image of the creator of all.

Where Christians are making conscious choices about sustained commitment to particular forms of work, it would therefore seem important to understand this as a matter of Christian vocation, and not simply as personal choice or an opportunity for self-fulfilment or self-expression. The truth is that we are bound to be formed to a very great extent through our work, perhaps more so than anything else apart from families of origin and present household relationships. The rhythms of our bodies, the habits of our hearts and the thinking of our minds will be decisively shaped through what we do day by day. It is a great privilege to be able to go out from the Eucharist into work where we can strive for objectives that speak of the goodness and faithfulness of God and return with both thanks and prayers that arise directly from what we have been doing. This is not primarily a matter of the particular job we are doing, so much as about how we engage with it; still, it is likely to be easier in some walks of life than others, and there may indeed be instances where it is hardly possible at all. Even where the fit seems relatively straightforward, there will be occasions when our experience of work begins to form us in habits of thinking and behaving that undermine our response to God's call. A large part of our Christian formation will be about how we negotiate the convergences and the tensions between the inevitably powerful secular formation that is happening through our work and our vocation to live in God's image, share in God's life and follow Jesus Christ day by day as workers, and not just as intermittent worshippers.

Alongside work, household relations also constitute a primary context for how we live out our Christian vocation. Can we talk here again about making conscious choices for distinctive forms of that vocation? This seems to me to be a potentially helpful way to frame the issues, not least because one of the striking things about Christians that we know from very early sources is that they did not believe that marriage was a way of life all should follow. There is no evidence that Jesus was married, and we have Paul's own word for it that he was not (1 Cor. 7.8). Against the assumptions of the ancient world as touched on in Chapter 3, Christians did not regard an unmarried person as somehow defective but rather able to testify in a distinctive way to the fullness of God's purposes. While this can and did become an unfortunate pretext for asserting the inferiority of the married life, it also opened up a new horizon in which marriage and celibacy alike could both be properly conceived as distinctive vocations within the life of faith.

As in the case of work, household relations can weave together the various strands we identified in our calling to be conformed to the image of God's Son: renewal of the purposes of human creation, disclosure of divine communion as our ground and end, and following the whole Christ with our whole lives. Home is itself a space of work for the sake of personal well-being and interpersonal relationships. In that work, we shape the physical environment of the home, undertake the tasks that sustain the life of the home and practise forms of community in daily relationships and the offering of hospitality. It is the place where we hope for times of release from all our work, and space for play and for rest. Our home may be marked by symbols and practices that reflect our participation in the life of the Church, witnessing to it and drawing others into it: grace before meals, family prayers, reading the Scriptures, a cross on the wall, the lighting of an Advent candle.

In both areas, we are made aware that the living out of Christian vocation does not depend simply on us, our desires and our decisions, but is always done in interdependence with others. We may feel strongly drawn to a particular kind of work or to a particular pattern of household relationships, such as marriage and parenthood; but we cannot realize these vocations without other people, nor indeed without the intersection of a whole range of factors lying beyond our direct control. We may find ourselves wanting to say at some point that the work we do and the household we inhabit in fact obstruct the fulfilment of our vocation – though we need to ask some careful questions in such cases before arriving at any conclusions. Our formation may take place through facing the failure of our hopes and yet holding on to the faithfulness of God who works our good in all things for us, which is that the purpose of our calling should be fulfilled.

Moreover, marriage and parenthood and indeed many kinds of work themselves bring responsibility for enabling others to find and fulfil their distinctive vocations in this life. Here too, response to God's call is not only from us and with others but also for the sake of others and their formation. Spouses are called to seek to enable the fullness of one another's vocation; parents to support their children as they begin to find theirs. What do we do when such responsibility appears to move us away from the kinds of activity that we had once thought to be primary ways in which we are to express our own Christian vocation? Parenthood may appear irreconcilable with both partners maintaining professional lives; the direction of work for one spouse may seem to require the other to focus on sustaining an income even if it means doing so through work that is felt to have no relation to that person's vocation. Once again, it is in the midst of such questions and struggles that Christian formation happens – or does not. Yes, we are formed by the Eucharist, by the worship of the Church, by the reading of the Scriptures and by prayer and meditation (as we will consider at greater length in the third part of the book) – but this is only one half of the whole. The other half is what happens in the rest of our lives, and if the two halves are separated from one another and do not feed into one another, our Christian formation will be a sickly thing at best.

Distinctive vocations: vocations of Christian ministry

Paul writes to the Corinthians about the rich variety of gifts, ministries and activities that are exchanged within the gathering of the Church there, to insist that as they come from the one Spirit so they should build up the Church as one body (1 Cor. 12.4–31). Ministry is not something that is restricted to a few individuals, but rather in its diversity reflects the abundance and freedom of the Holy Spirit, 'who allots to each one individually just as the Spirit chooses' (1 Cor. 12.11). The New Testament also 'however' describes particular people as ministers and indicates that it was a practice from early times to discern in some people a particular ministerial identity. 1 Corinthians 12.28 lists apostles, prophets and teachers, to which Ephesians 4.11 adds evangelists and pastors; Acts and Paul's letters to Timothy give us overseers (from which we derive the word 'bishops'), presbyters (from which we get 'priests') and deacons.[43] Other passages suggest other roles as well; clearly terminology and practice varied across different communities. Yet we might

---

43 For presbysters, one of the most widely attested roles in New Testament Christianity, see e.g. Acts 11.30, 14.23, 16.4, 20.17–35; 1 Tim. 5.17–22; Titus 1.5; James 5.14; 1 Peter 5.1–5; 2 John 1; 3 John 1. For deacons, see e.g. Phil. 1.1; 1 Tim. 3.8–13; and for overseers/bishops, e.g. Phil. 1.1; 1 Tim. 3.1–7; Titus 1.7–9.

venture that two things have been relatively constant factors since earliest times. First, for every person in the Church, one way in which the response to Christ's call can be expressed is through particular gifts of ministry that build up the body of Christ. Second, for some people, that response will be expressed through an open-ended and potentially lifelong commitment to a distinctive form of ministry, such that it sets the parameters for their place in the life of the Church. For these people, Christian vocation becomes bound to ministerial vocation, and Christian formation to ministerial formation.

Such distinctive forms of ministry derive from the pattern of the Church's life that we have been describing in this chapter. For the different parts of the Church to work in harmony together with all their diverse gifts, there needs to be some kind of co-ordination that enables all of this wonderful activity to move together towards the one goal of maturity in Christ (Eph. 4.11–16). For there to be a baptism, someone must administer it; for there to be a Eucharist, someone must preside. Moreover, for there to be a baptism, someone must oversee instruction in the faith given to candidates, and for there to be any candidates in the first place apart from the children of believers, someone must be ensuring that the gospel message is shared with those who have not received it in a way that is both truthful and accessible. Similarly, for there to be a Eucharist, someone must preach from the Scriptures, and to feed the formation of the people in their daily vocation there needs to be teaching both here and in other contexts as well. This group of Christians that assembles week by week and also perhaps in smaller numbers day by day needs certain resources: a place to gather, a font for baptism, a table for the Eucharist, a collection for the poor and some means to maintain and distribute it, and a copy of the Scriptures. Because this group is the Church, it is also part of the Church: it belongs within the body of Christ that reaches across the world, so it needs some means of relating to Churches in other places too. That body extends through time as well as space, and the group of Christians will therefore need to know its place within a tradition that stretches back to the apostles and the prophets.

Why do we have ordained ministers in the life of the Church? The answer must be to do with these responsibilities that arise from the actions that make the Church what it is as the shared response to God's call through Christ. Once we move beyond this point, however, we quickly enter difficult territory historically and theologically; indeed, the difficulty is in part the way that the history of ministry has often been written to provide theological justification for current practice in some Churches and to disparage the practices of others. Although there have been significant developments towards an ecumenical theology of ministry and scholarly convergence on some points of history at least, substantial agreement remains elusive and much work remains to be done.[44] In what follows, therefore, I try to focus on a few points about ordained ministry as distinctive vocation that seem to me to be particularly relevant for understanding what kind of formation might be needed for it. I realize that this means writing in very general terms without distinguishing different orders of ministry, as most Churches do. I hope, however, that it will be sufficient to indicate how such vocations might be understood within the context of the shared vocation of the Church, and how ministerial formation might be approached within the overarching context of Christian formation.

First, the tradition which has been received from the early centuries is that responsibility for the tasks that need doing for the Church to be itself is best given to particular people who freely commit themselves to accepting an appropriate form of that responsibility for life. That means there is a very

---

44 See for instance Stephen Pickard, 2009, *Theological Foundations for Collaborative Ministry*, Farnham: Ashgate.

serious decision to be made by both the person concerned and the Church which asks that person to accept it. It is a decision that needs to be made in freedom and also without reservation. Like the promises of baptism and of marriage, it is a commitment to living one's life in a particular way whose outcomes are not predictable. This makes it strange in a culture in which the contract is becoming a dominant model for human relationships within the assumptions of egoism (as reviewed in Chapter 3): I commit myself to doing something for you for as long as the outcomes for both of us are satisfactory. Vocation to ordained ministry is by contrast about a commitment to letting my life be shaped by specific responsibilities in the life of the Church, with no opt-out clauses on either side.

Second, the open-ended commitment implied in accepting orders of ministry is lived out in limited and specific offices of ministerial responsibility. Orders are for life, and for every day of our lives; offices are for set periods of time, including potentially set days of the week, and they may even be framed by a formal contract of employment or something very like one. Any office in the Church should be received with a deep sense of gratitude and privilege, but it is also a piece of work and therefore shares in all the complex dynamics that we were describing in the previous section. To expect work for Christian ministry to be somehow protected from the challenges and pressures of ordinary, 'secular' work is deeply foolhardy. Work is always secular in the weak sense of that word set out in Part 1 of this book: it binds us to the patterns of economic, social and cultural life in the particular age in which we are living. Moreover, work in the Church is just as capable of enmeshing us in sin and in the age that is passing away as work in any other human context. It is just that the temptations are likely to be somewhat different. So everything that was said about formation through work in the previous section applies just as much to ordained ministers.

Third, most clergy outside the Roman Catholic Church are combining a vocation to ordained ministry with a vocation to marriage, which itself entails a commitment to support the unfolding vocation of one's spouse, as has been said; some are also maintaining a distinctive vocation to paid employment in a different context. They are therefore likely to face questions about how the commitments and responsibilities implied in these different vocations cohere with one another and to experience times when they seem to conflict sharply. Formation for vocation needs to attend very carefully to these issues: no vocation to ordained ministry is lived apart from the whole life of the person, and therefore neither will the various dimensions of formation happen in isolation. In particular, there is bound to be a strong influence from formation through work and household relations on formation for and in ministry. On the other hand, where formation for ministry leads to strong personal and spiritual growth, there is likely to be a feedback effect in turn on the person's engagement with work and household, which may be received there as positive but may also be experienced as difficult and disruptive. If Christian formation is always about the person, it cannot in truth be otherwise.

Fourth, while it is not helpful to see formation as just for the clergy, a vocation to ordained ministry implies a particular need for shaping by the Holy Spirit in order to respond, and a continual need for such shaping in order to sustain our response. As I will try to explain more fully in the following part of the book, understanding Christian formation as the work of the Holy Spirit does not mean it makes no demand on us in terms of attention, discipline and work. There is therefore wisdom in the tradition that expects those whom the Church believes may be called to this ministry to withdraw, to some degree or another, from present responsibilities in congregational life to focus on making space for their deeper formation as set out in the next part of this book, alongside activities that allow them to explore the responsibilities that they will be assuming. Ministerial formation as such is about the way that an intensified engagement with Christian formation of the person interacts with sustained consideration of the specific character of the ministry in the Church to which we believe we are being called.[45]

Finally, I said in the previous section that some vocations of daily life, including marriage and parenthood, required supporting the vocations of others as one of their inherent components. This would also be true in a powerful way of a distinctive vocation to ordained ministry. To accept orders of ministry is to receive, as a lifelong charge, responsibility for guiding other Christians in their vocation and for feeding them for the formation that follows from this. Christian formation is indeed the work of the Holy Spirit, but it happens in human contexts over which some people have more power than others, and clergy generally have more power than most. Beyond the particular activities in which they are likely to be involved that have a relatively direct bearing on the formation of Christians, as already noted in passing it is the 'micro-culture' of the congregation that will have a huge bearing on how these activities are actually experienced and what kind of messages they actually convey.[46] Clergy do not create this local culture by themselves yet they have considerable scope for influencing it and a clear responsibility for shaping it so that it does indeed nurture Christian formation within the particular and unique context of a congregation's life. It is because their distinctive vocation commits them to the complex task of supporting the formation of Christian communities that attending to what it

---

45 Jeremy Worthen, 2008, 'A Model of Ministerial Formation: Conceptual Framework and Practical Implications', in Angela Shier-Jones (ed.), *The Making of Ministry*, Peterborough: Epworth, pp. 38–54.

46 Denham Grierson, 1984, *Transforming a People of God*, Melbourne: The Joint Board of Christian Education of Australia and New Zealand.

means to be in formation is so vital for ordained ministers – beginning with themselves.

Chapter review

The purpose of our calling can be summed up as becoming conformed to the Son of God, which means renewal of the image in which we were created, participation in God's eternal life and following Jesus day by day. Our response to this calling comes from us as human persons, with others in the life of the Church and for others, not just in the Church but the whole world. The two sacraments of baptism and Eucharist have a unique place in shaping this response, and as the primary practices of the Church they communicate the gospel's paradoxical narrative of human fulfilment through death and resurrection. Within the shared response of the Church, marriage and celibacy, as well as work, can become distinctive vocations that frame faith's daily answer to God's call. Ordained ministry is also properly considered a vocation in a parallel way. In each case, distinctive vocations generate particular challenges and opportunities for Christian formation.

PART 3

Making Space for Christian Formation

In the first part of this book, I tried to draw out a few strands from the complex and interwoven mass of ways in which we have been and continue to be formed by participation in the world. To be human is to be constantly shaped by our experienced context, from our earliest beginnings onwards, and to be at the same time shaping that context through our own response to it. Formation as such, then, is not something we have a choice about: formation has happened, is happening and will continue to happen as long as we live, and in it we are neither slaves nor masters, neither passive recipients nor wholly autonomous beings able to impose our self-created will on ourselves or others.

In the second part of the book, I wanted to establish some theological foundations for Christian formation by reflecting on vocation. God's call in creation is renewed and restated in Christ, and its purpose revealed as becoming conformed to the image of God's eternal Son. Our response to this call comes from us, from our inmost being, but it is also always made with others in the life of the Church and for the sake of others, that they too might hear God's call and be drawn into the fullness of God's purpose. The interwoven sacraments of baptism and Eucharist draw us into the reality of this communion, show us the fullness of its meaning and summon us to live it day by day in the world. As they give the pattern for Christian vocation, they are also the primary context for our formation: we are shaped for and in our 'Yes' to Christ in baptism, our regular participation in the assembly of the Church for thanksgiving, prayer, word and sacrament and our daily journey of discipleship marked by witness and service.

Within that primary context, we make decisions about lifelong or at least long-term commitments that set further specific parameters for how we respond to God's call, in terms of work, relationships and ministry. Where we can recognize and own such decisions as relating to the overarching purpose of our calling as becoming conformed to the image of God's Son, we can speak about such commitments as distinctive vocations within the shared vocation of the Church. These distinctive vocations, as expressions of our response to God's call, then become a secondary context for our formation. They are commitments that will, inevitably, shape us, but if we make them also commitments to seeking the purpose of God in our lives, with others and for the sake of others, they can shape us in and for our vocation in Christ and contribute decisively to our Christian formation.

If all that is true, is it not unnecessary to make formation a matter of deliberate focus, let alone effort for us? There are two ways in which this question might be put. The first would be on the grounds that our attention should be fixed on acting in response to God's call, and we should simply trust that formation will be taking place as we are faithful in discipleship and ministry. There is some validity to this, yet there are also different seasons in the life of discipleship, and in some of them we will be especially aware that our current 'shaping' as persons inhibits our ability to respond to God's call and do the work that God has given us. One such season might be – perhaps should be – that of preparation to take on a major responsibility in the life of the Church, such as ordained ministry, and the first few

100

steps into that responsibility with its heightened levels of both authority and accountability. Another would be preparation for baptism, first Communion or confirmation, and the first steps into that new level of sharing in the body of Christ. Nor is this only about beginnings: in our continuing participation in the shared vocation of the Church as well as in our distinctive vocations, there are likely to be moments when we recognize that aspects of what we have become through our secular vocation are seriously inhibiting our fruitfulness and perhaps faithfulness. In a social and ecclesiastical context where anxiety generates a reflex of activism, it is particularly vital to see these seasons not as distractions from the real business of discipleship but as openings for the purpose according to which we were called: becoming conformed as persons to God's Word, so that the Word might dwell richly in us (Col. 3.16) and speak powerfully through us.

Another way of raising the question about the need for us to attend to Christian formation might be to ask who is doing the work here. Is it not the Holy Spirit who forms us, and indeed who forms Christ in us (Gal. 4.19; cf. Col. 1.27)? Again, we need to say 'Yes, but'. Yes, and we should therefore show some reservation in talking about human individuals and organizations as agents of Christian formation. But this is not to indulge the idea that the Holy Spirit only works through private and spontaneous experiences granted to special individuals. The Holy Spirit is given by Christ to the Church, his body: the communion of believers in Christ with one another and with the Triune God. It is, then, through human relationships within the life of the Church that the Holy Spirit is at work in Christian formation. Within those relationships, some people, as we suggested at the end of the previous chapter, will be called to responsibilities that pertain specifically to this. Still, we should remain reluctant to speak of Christian formation, or indeed ministerial formation as one kind of Christian formation, as something that some Christians do to others. It is the work of the Holy Spirit among us, within us and between us.

Hence the title of this third part: making space for Christian formation. At the heart of any seeking after Christian formation must be prayer: a waiting on the Holy Spirit to come and restore God's image within us, lead us deeper into communion with the Triune creator and bestow on us the gifts that we need to follow Jesus day by day. Waiting, however, does not mean the absence of activity or effort. If we want to grow in the fullness of response to God's call to us, we need to work at making space for the work of the Holy Spirit in forming us. God's desire is to act with, not against, our freedom and our freely undertaken efforts. That is part of what it means to be made in God's image and likeness.

What might this involve? In the three chapters that follow, I have used one of Augustine's models for the image of the God who is Trinity in the human mind: the interlinked activities of remembering, understanding and willing. This model, along with a number of variations, appears in his great work *On the Trinity* and is used by many different writers in subsequent traditions of Western Christianity. Although it has not been without its critics, it still seems to me to provide a helpful framework for thinking through what 'the renewing of our minds' (Rom. 12.2) might mean. In particular, it enables us to revisit the themes of freedom, knowledge and love from Part 1 and ask how the insights of Christian theology and the currents of our culture meet together in the spaces we make for our formation. It also urges us to see remembering, understanding and willing as inseparable from one another, woven together in love, and that too will, I hope, become apparent as we focus on each in turn.

Each chapter begins by sketching out the place of the activity we are considering within Christian formation: how are memory, understanding and will formed, in the light of the theological work presented in Part 2 and the analysis of late modern culture in Part 1? We then proceed to focus on a particular dimension of making space for Christian formation 'with others' – in the local congregation, in small groups of disciples, in communities of ministry students and staff, in Christian institutions and organizations more widely and indeed in the Christian home. In relation to remembering, we reflect on liturgical formation; in relation to understanding, on theological formation; and in relation to willing, on moral formation. I realize that some readers may be disappointed by the lack of detailed prescriptions about how to 'do' formation in the particular context that concerns them, such as the congregation or seminary, but I hope to set out some parameters and principles that can support work across the variety of settings within which we need to be making space for Christian formation. No single context can take the entire weight here.

In the third section of each chapter, we turn to some of the challenges and difficulties that are likely to arise in any sustained attempt to make space for formation by the Holy Spirit. Deep changes to our acquired habits of remembering, understanding and willing will not come quickly or easily, and at times it may seem that even the progress we thought we had made is crumbling away before us. Finally, we consider spiritual formation in terms of practices through which we seek to make space for the Holy Spirit to transform us in our uniqueness at the deepest level, using three traditional concepts from Christian spirituality: meditation, contemplation and election.

7

Remembering

Forming our memory

Formation for vocation rests on our deepening remembrance of who God is for us and who we are before God. Our calling is to live by faith in the faithful one, and there is no recognition of faithfulness without remembrance. To know God as faithful is to remember that we have always been living at God's hand, that this God who once called us is the same God who calls us today and that the Word does not falter or fail: 'Jesus Christ is the same yesterday and today and for ever' (Heb. 13.8). And Jesus sends the Holy Spirit to form us by keeping in our memory everything that he has said and leading us into the fullness of its meaning (John 14.26).

Christian vocation is bound up with promising: God's promises to us, and our promises to God in the presence of the Church and to one another in the presence of God. Vocation flows from the fulfilment of God's promises, and though, as we said in Chapter 5, there is always more in the fulfilment than we could have anticipated from the promise, nonetheless it is only by remembering the promise that we can begin to understand the fulfilment. In baptism, we pledge ourselves to reject evil and follow the way of Christ, and the whole of our life in Christ follows from this promise. The Eucharist is both remembrance of God's 'Yes' in Christ to all that has been promised, and remembrance of our own commitment in baptism to life in Christ.

Everything we do in the name of Christ, in response to the call of Christ, finds its source and its renewal here.

Remembering, then, is fundamental to Christian formation: not the memory of what happened 'once upon a time' or in the distant past, but the active calling to mind of how God has called us and how we have responded as the defining contours for our today, for our reality. Christians live, we might say, in the perfect tense: who we are and shall be is determined by what God has said and how we have answered. Yet this rooting of selfhood in remembrance is not easy. That is in part because our secular formation as described in Part 1 works relatively directly against it. Expressive individualism teaches us that true selfhood is about what we make and create now, what springs up from our own originality. It is a message to which are constantly exposed, when we turn on the TV, watch a film, read a novel, pick up a self-help book, go on a training course at work or notice an advertisement out of the corner of our eye on the street or screen. We are exposed to it not just by the content of such communication but by its manner, constantly changing and shifting and celebrating a lack of continuity between past and present, the irrelevance of memory to meaning, which is something we must keep creating afresh for ourselves.

This cultural environment that promotes the detachment of memory from meaning can appear to be reinforced by the influence of technology on our self-understanding, fed in particular by the pervasiveness of computers in our physical environment and by the promise of research in Artificial Intelligence.[47] If we imagine ourselves as computer-like minds in soft-tissue bodies, it seems obvious to think of memory as a place in the brain where information goes to be stored automatically, and in which we

---

47 World Council of Churches, 2005, *Christian Perspectives on Theological Anthropology: A Faith and Order Study Document*, Faith and Order Paper 199, Geneva: WCC, pp. 30–1.

then rummage around in order to retrieve it for specific purposes. Meaning becomes something we do with memory, as if remembering itself were a wholly mechanistic process.

Contrary to this picture of memory as a kind of receptacle into which stuff somehow finds its way of its own accord, remembering is always an interpretive activity in which we are involved. Just as there is in fact no way to store data on a computer without some kind of work by human minds at some point to organize that data, so there is no way that our minds can remember things without some kind of activity by those minds in interpreting the world we experience. Remembering is in fact inseparable from how we make sense of the world, and making sense of the world is what human beings do as meaning-making organisms.[48] We do not remember things and then, as a secondary move, make sense of them; we are always already making sense of things as we remember them, by the way that we remember them.

Indeed, paradoxical as it may sound, we can only remember if we also forget. To remember, we have to bring some things into focus in the foreground, and let others fall relatively neglected into the background. When we describe someone's memory as 'selective' we usually intend it as a criticism, meaning they have deliberately forgotten inconvenient facts. Yet all memory is necessarily selective. There is a wonderful and terrifying short story by the Argentine writer Jorge Luis Borges called 'Funes the Memorious', about a man who loses the ability to forget after falling off his horse and suffering a serious head injury.[49] Its description of a man who cannot forget anything at all, not even the most fleeting impression glimpsed out of the corner of his eye or on the far horizon, represents rigorously

---

48 Robert Kegan, 1982, *The Evolving Self: Problem and Process in Human Development*, Cambridge, Massachusetts: Harvard University Press, p. 11.

49 Jorge Luis Borges, 1970, 'Funes the Memorious', in *Labyrinths: Selected Stories and Other Writings*, Harmondsworth: Penguin, pp. 87–95.

non-selective remembering, what we might call 'total memory', as a kind of nightmare. It is by remembering some things as more significant than others that I am able to interpret what has happened to me as my past, my story, and not become wholly lost or submerged in it. Where memory (hypothetically and unimaginably) cannot select, as in Funes' case, and therefore cannot interpret, human selfhood becomes unsustainable.

The link that arises from this work of fiction between memory, selection and interpretation is also an important theme in cognitive psychology, where it has been argued on the basis of extensive empirical studies that human beings are always 'framing' their experience in narrative forms. We might compare the way that the media seems to work with certain standard stories, for instance about church divisions over sex, reporting avidly anything that can be made to fit one of them and displaying little interest in what cannot. In a parallel fashion, in the mind of the individual person 'what does *not* get structured narratively suffers loss in memory. Framing pursues experience into memory.'[50] We remember what fits the various 'scripts' we carry with us; what does not catch on them is likely to slip through memory's mesh, while what clashes harshly may sometimes stand out as something we cannot comprehend. The point here is that it is naïve to imagine we could 'just' remember without having some kind of prior script to help us discern what matters for us and what does not. We remember what happens to us in the light of stories that are deeply woven into our minds, which allow us to receive experience as meaningful and significant rather than utterly and destructively random.

Once we grasp the insight that remembering is an interpretive activity in which we are constantly engaged and indeed at some level constantly making choices, then we can begin to

---

50 Jerome Bruner, 1990, *Acts of Meaning*, Cambridge, Massachusetts: Harvard University Press, p. 56 (italics in original).

understand why it is so crucial in making space for formation. As we say yes to God's call, we come to remember our own story as standing within the whole story of God and humanity, of our calling in creation renewed through Christ, to which we respond with and for others in the Church. And as we remember that story more and more fully, so we may begin to draw on it more and more deeply for the scripts that shape the way we receive what we experience as happening to us and therefore frame how we act and respond.

It is hard to place remembrance of the faithfulness of God at the heart of our sense of selfhood in a culture that combines the good news of expressive individualism with mechanistic pictures of the human mind. Yet part of the story that we remember is that this has never been easy. In the book of Exodus, we read about how, having called Israel out of Egypt and into the land promised to Abraham, God does not take the Hebrews straight there but first hardens the heart of Pharaoh and then leads them through a long sojourn in the wilderness. God's purpose here is formation: Israel is being shaped so that a people may enter the land who are ready to respond to God's word, God's speech. And their formation on the way from the Red Sea to the Jordan pivots on remembering, on learning to remember God and themselves in a way that will sustain them in living their vocation on the other side.

It begins before the people leave Egypt. As Moses prepares them for the last and most deadly of the plagues, he instructs them in the rituals of the Passover. At this decisive moment, as the people of Israel await God's deliverance, they are told to remember: 'This day shall be a day of remembrance for you. You shall celebrate it as a festival to the Lord; throughout your generations you shall observe it as a perpetual ordinance' (Ex. 12.14). Remembering, in this context, does not mean making sure one thinks about something from time to time: it is about commitment to repeated participation in a corporate ritual at regular intervals. Remembering is an embodied activity, not just a matter of mental attention. Observing the details of the ritual is how the people will remember this night of all nights: 'Remember this day on which you came out of Egypt, out of the house of slavery, because the Lord brought you out from there by strength of hand; no leavened bread shall be eaten' (Ex. 13.3).

The first word that Moses brings down from Sinai for the Israelites is not a command, but an introduction to all God's commands that tells them who is the one who is speaking by reminding them what this one has done for them. 'Then God spoke all these words: "I am the Lord your God, who brought you out of the land of Egypt, out of the house of slavery: you shall have no other gods before me"' (Ex. 20.1). We cannot hear the commands without remembering who gave them and the story of divine faithfulness that joins us with this past today. Indeed, the fourth of the Ten Commandments given to Moses is explicitly about remembering: 'Remember the sabbath day, and keep it holy' (Ex. 20.8). In Exodus, remembering the Sabbath day through the practice of rest is tied to recalling that 'in six days the Lord made heaven and earth, the sea and all that is in them, but rested the seventh day' (Ex. 20.11) – faith in God as creator. In Deuteronomy, it is linked instead to faith in God as liberator and provokes a further, explicit command to remember: 'Remember that you were a slave in the land of Egypt, and the Lord your God brought you out from there with a mighty hand and an outstretched arm; therefore the Lord commanded you to keep the sabbath day' (Deut. 5.15). Remembering who we are before God and who God is for us is something that requires the people of Israel to learn some very specific practices about the keeping and hallowing of time. It calls for a discipline that will shape the rhythm of their lives, constantly interrupting days of work and activity with space for remembering God as creator and liberator.

The relationship between the command to remember and the keeping of commands for the sake of remembering emerges as a major theme in the book of Deuteronomy. The literary context here is Moses addressing the people one last time before he dies as they prepare finally to cross the Jordan. This gives a particular urgency to his repeated command to remember and not forget what has happened to them up to this point: the deliverance from Egypt, the revelation at Sinai/Horeb and the journey through the wilderness (Deut. 4.9). Once settled in the land, it will be easy to forget the God who did these things, but the whole purpose of the commands given at Sinai/Horeb is explained in terms of ensuring that this God is not forgotten (Deut. 6.4–25). Keeping the commandments of the Torah ties every 'today' to the day of God's speaking to Moses at Horeb: 'Not with our ancestors did the Lord make this covenant, but with us, who are all of us here alive today' (Deut. 5.3). To respond to the call of God as expressed through the teaching of the Law, Israel must be formed in continual remembrance of how it was given and thereby of the giver of this binding gift.

Liturgical formation

What then of Christians today, who do not follow the Torah of Sinai in its entirety or keep Passover as such? How do we make space for the formation of our memory, given that the challenges here have not diminished over the centuries? The Old Testament speaks of a need for shared rhythms of ritual and recitation in order for our remembering to be constantly renewed and the good news of God's gracious deliverance not allowed to become forgotten. Ultimately, the early Church withdrew from the shared rhythms of Judaism that had been developed over time from the teaching in the Pentateuch and grew instead its own distinctive patterns of remembrance that nonetheless were laid over and across those earlier rhythms. These patterns, expressed in common worship, have shaped the fabric of Christian life for two millennia and been critical for Christian formation through establishing its roots in remembering. Yet perhaps they are under threat today as never before. We will return to this point in a moment, but first we need to sketch out the patterns themselves and say something about how they originated.

It is not easy to do this briefly, as there are complex scholarly debates about the beginnings of what became normal practice in Christian worship.[51] Nonetheless, if we consider what we know about Christian life in the major cities of the Roman empire towards the end of the fourth century, we can see a great deal of common ground with later Christianity extending up to our own time. Daily prayer, ideally with others, is considered to be part of the bedrock of Christian discipleship. It involves the remembrance of God's goodness in praise and thanksgiving, and the remembrance too of our needs and failings and indeed those of the whole world in prayer. Such daily remembrance is fed by the faithful reading of the Scriptures, with a special place given to the Psalms as biblical words which can become our words, our speech before God.[52] Christians gather every week on Sunday for the Eucharist, which as we said in the previous chapter brings together thanksgiving, the hearing of God's word through Scripture and its exposition, a common meal in memory of the present Christ and sending out for service and witness in the world for which we continually pray. Over this basic rhythm of daily and weekly remembrance in worship is laid the counterpoint of yearly cycles, of which the oldest revolves around what we call Easter, which for the early

---

51 Paul F. Bradshaw, 2002, *The Search for the Origins of Christian Worship: Sources and Methods for the Study of Early Liturgy*, 2nd edn, London: SPCK.

52 Dietrich Bonhoeffer, 1970, *Psalms: The Prayer Book of the Bible*, ET, Minneapolis, Minnesota: Augsburg.

Christians was simply their 'Passover', parallel to that of their Jewish neighbours, in which they celebrated every year their deliverance through Christ from sin, death and slavery.

For Christians too, then, remembering has been shared, embodied, symbolic activity, which structures their years, their weeks and their days. Liturgists talk about *anamnesis* (the Greek term for remembrance) as a fundamental dimension of all Christian worship, which brings the assembly of believers into the present reality of that which we remember as God's work.[53] It is through this continual shared practice of *anamnesis* that my personal remembering can be shaped in the light of divine teaching and I can learn how to tell my unique, unrepeatable story as one strand in the story of amazing grace that reaches from creation to redemption and encompasses all things in the one mystery of Christ crucified and risen. The foundation of Christian formation has been liturgical formation, the shaping of all our remembrance through the common rhythms of assembling for worship as the Church.[54]

I have already noted, however, that these rhythms look increasingly fragile in our contemporary cultural context. Even among those who identify as Christian and attend worship regularly, participation every Sunday may be regarded as less than a major priority and engagement with anything in the calendar beyond Easter and Christmas purely optional, with structured daily prayer an aspiration for the devout rather than a basic Christian discipline. The dislocations between love and duty, the personal and the

---

53 Julie Gittoes, 2008, *Anamnesis and the Eucharist: Contemporary Anglican Approaches*, Aldershot: Ashgate, pp. 9–31.

54 In this chapter, my focus is on how we are formed through participation in liturgy, rather than how we might need to be formed for such participation. For an analysis of the somewhat complex term 'liturgical formation', which can encompass both of these, see Christopher Irvine, 2005, *The Art of God: The Making of Christians and the Meaning of Worship*, London: SPCK, pp. 63–90.

corporate, explored back in Part 1 are certainly part of the picture here: I need to find *my* way to express *my* faith, and following with others received patterns of prayer, worship and Bible reading does not seem a likely way to achieve that. There are other factors at work here too. The notion of daily and yearly cycles made natural sense in a predominantly agricultural society. Large-scale urban ization, industrialization and the spread of new technologies – from the clock to the electric light – insulate us from the kind of intense awareness of times and seasons possessed by the vast majority of our forebears.[55] Moreover, modernity itself tends to make time homogenous, all of a piece: the celebration of 'festive' times, understood as drawing us towards the 'higher' times from which our ordinary time flows, has been criticized since the six-teenth century as both irrational, indeed superstitious, and economically unproductive – initially by reforming Christians. We are encouraged to see time as a thing that we have an obliga-tion to use and make the most of, not a space within which we share with both the living and the dead in weaving a tapestry of eternity as gathered time from all of our unique threads.[56]

It is not hard to see that public liturgy as shared *anamnesis* is at many levels a foreign language in late modernity.[57] Yet it is also a language that is more critical than ever for the work of Christian formation. Participation in liturgy that draws on authorized texts and is based on sources from centuries of tradition reminds us that vocation is something we receive from God with others, in other congregations, cities and countries today and from other ages and places across history. It is not our creation, nor is it our

---

55 Doctrine Commission of the General Synod of the Church of England, 2003, *Being Human: A Christian Understanding of Personhood Illustrated with Reference to Power, Money, Sex and Time*, London: Church House Publishing, pp. 102–6.

56 Charles Taylor, 2007, *A Secular Age*, Cambridge, Massachusetts: Belknap Press, pp. 54–9.

57 Irvine, *Art of God*, p. 86.

particular possession: it is God's gift that has been offered to all and has been taken up by many, and our response is always and necessarily a response in companionship with others from the past as well as the present. It reminds us also that this calling we have received is not just for us, not just for those who gather with us, but for the world. Intercession for the world is not optional, and therefore remembrance of the tragedies and traumas of the world is not optional either. Remembrance of the poor and the oppressed is not optional. Remembrance of all that stands in contradiction to the good news we are bound to proclaim is not optional. Without such remembrance, the gospel can slip into a false promise of emotional and even material security that denies reality and will sound fearfully hollow to the broken and the outcast who were the particular focus of Jesus' own concern.

This is not to succumb again to prevailing dichotomies. Liturgy does not and should not mean the discouragement of creativity and imagination: its patterns mean we have a score, but no musical performer thinks that just following the notes is all that is needed. The performance of classical music, like more traditional forms of liturgy, requires a depth of knowledge and an edge of flair in interpreting familiar works. The performance of jazz and other styles, like more consciously contemporary approaches to liturgy, requires thorough awareness of forms, patterns and structures and acute listening to the activity of others, as well as hard-practised creativity, in order to make something that is at once new and of the moment yet also recognizably in continuity with tradition. It is true that liturgy is almost bound to need to move somewhat towards the 'jazz' end of the spectrum of this analogy if it is to be hospitable to people whose secular formation is in late modern culture. If so, the demands on those who prepare and oversee public worship need to be recognized. In a classical idiom, competent if uninspiring performance of the text is just about acceptable: a lack of any great talent need not prevent the music from being heard. Once an improvisatory element is taken for granted, a different and much more direct onus of responsibility is laid on those who lead, and they need very thorough training in some quite different skills from their predecessors. The implications of this for the formation of those who take responsibility for the Church's gathering for worship are far-reaching.

Finally, it is perhaps worth stressing that the reading of Scripture has always been central for Christian liturgy, indeed that Scripture is the primary text for Christian liturgy. The transposition of that text into the shifting rhythms of liturgical remembrance was achieved through following a common lectionary, originally within a diocese but then more widely. Although some Protestant churches initially rejected this in the sixteenth century – though not the Church of England – the twenty-first has seen the spread of more or less common lectionary provision across a wide range of denominations and indeed continents. There is a wonderful opportunity here for shared formation in remembrance as we hear Scripture read and preached. Liturgy should foster our remembering of our whole life within the whole story of God's call to the whole world, and attention to Scripture in its breadth as well as its depth is vital to this. We need to be formed in remembering what God has spoken as witnessed in the totality of the Old and New Testaments, and in their constant and sometimes puzzling juxtaposition. On the eve of the Second World War, Bonhoeffer was defending the practice of reading extensive passages from both the Old and New Testaments together in continuous sequence as part of daily common worship, against those who saw it as information overload and leaving insufficient scope for individual reflection. 'Only in so far as we are *there*, is God with us today also', he wrote.[58] Something very precious is lost when such reading

---

58 Dietrich Bonhoeffer, 1954, *Life Together*, ET, London: SCM, p. 44 (italics in original).

becomes a private matter only, and the diet for public reading and preaching becomes restricted to a relatively narrow selection of passages decided by individual ministers and congregations.

Fractured memory

As we began to see in the first section of this chapter, the emergence of human selfhood as analysed by modern psychology is inextricably bound up with memory. The sense of a continuous self depends on the existence of an 'I' in the present that can identify with a sequence of memories receding into the past. This is not something that we are simply born with, however. On the contrary, it is something that has to be achieved by the young child, in collaboration with the humans who care for it, by passing through a number of distinct stages, within which the acquisition of language forms a critical part.[59] With language, the child learns to name itself as a distinct entity within its horizons of perception. It also learns to attribute to itself desires, actions and feelings. Finally, it starts to tell its story – perhaps better in the first place its stories, which only gradually are brought together through remembering into a single story that can become my story, my 'self'. The pre-schooler sitting up in bed and rehearsing out loud what it did today before going to sleep is not simply engaging in a performance that eavesdropping adults might find charming. He or she is 'practising' selfhood through the kind of narrative activity that builds particular memories into something approaching continuous sequence, a sequence somehow threatened through its imminent interruption in sleep.

For better or worse, however, we are not able to recall these first stages of our selfhood. There is a kind of line or barrier that

---

59 Charles Ferneyhough, 2008, *The Baby in the Mirror: A Child's World from Birth to Three*, London: Granta, pp. 129–64.

separates the self that is generally established by the age of five or six from remembering most of what preceded it. Reflection on this barrier has been particularly significant for what is sometimes called depth psychology, i.e. approaches to modern psychology that follow Freud in understanding the mind as a dynamic interplay between conscious and unconscious activities. For them, memories held unconsciously are critical for my sense of selfhood. The primary 'scripts' (to return to a term we used earlier) that frame how I understand myself, how I develop as a person and how I engage with others are not normally accessible to my conscious mind. Hence they are bound to remain for the most part impervious to even the most whole-hearted conscious engagement with the beliefs and practices of the Christian Church. If that is right, then it would seem that no amount of participation in the liturgy, however wonderful it may be, can revisit and reset the tracks of memory that were set in those early childhood years. Christian formation can only shape our remembering in relatively superficial ways. The best hope for deeper change, it might be argued, lies with the psychotherapist.

Now, it would be easy to shrug off this challenge by pointing to the huge army of critics of depth psychology, both inside and outside the field of psychology. Moreover, it is also true that within depth psychology itself there are contrasting views on how the power of unconscious affective memories over our conscious behaviour might be addressed in adulthood, from the pessimism of Freud to the greater optimism of Jung and Erikson. It is also the case that Freud was an overt critic of Christianity and indeed of all forms of Christian faith, so it is tempting to treat him simply as an adversary rather than someone from whom we might learn. Yet it seems to me that for all the waning of Freud's direct influence since the mid-twentieth century, it is a challenge we still need to take seriously.

This is in part because Freud's core idea has an appeal that does not depend on accepting all the apparatus of his psychological speculation: the emotional power of particular memories, including those we gained in early childhood, continues to affect us even (and indeed especially) when we cannot readily recall the particular memories themselves in the present. The appeal here is not only in the idea's potential relevance for therapeutic practice, but also in its richness for both the arts and philosophy in their exploration of human selfhood. Indeed, it is an idea that has very deep roots in Western culture, from Plato's teaching that knowledge means remembering the truths that we can only recall through the therapy of philosophy, through Augustine's fascination with the paradoxes of memory in Book X of the *Confessions*, to Proust's exploration of 'involuntary memory' in his monumental novel.

We might summarize all this by saying that depth psychology suggests that a book like this on Christian formation can foster unrealistic expectations about people's ability to change through intentional activity, because it does not reckon with the abiding power of our deepest, unconscious memories. As such, it is likely to lead to disappointment, breeding resentment, despair or both. So is there really any point in making space for formation through disciplines of remembrance?

We are called to grow into the fullness of God's purpose through time, and therefore to take time to be formed for our calling. That this journey should span our lifetime and even beyond should hardly be surprising; that sin means the goal will always elude us before our death but still find us by God's grace at the resurrection of the dead is historic Christian orthodoxy. Depth psychology represents a secular language that is not necessarily at odds with many of the traditional themes of Christian spirituality in grappling with the limits of transformation by the Holy Spirit in the present age. To be an embodied creature who is also spirit is to be something of incredible intricacy, whose history is bound up with its being in ways which we cannot finally fathom. The critique from depth psychology can therefore be heard as a corrective to forms of Christian teaching that forget these depths for the sake of a superficial and optimistic view of human nature that owes much more to modern fantasies of self-creation than to the sources of Christian tradition.

The connecting memory that is the fragile growth of our earliest years and remains fractured by the divide between conscious and unconscious activity will utterly fail for all of us sooner or later; that is the reality of life in the shadows of sin. Yet the limits of our ability to remember who God is for us and who we are before God and to be formed by that remembering do not stop God being who God is for us and therefore us being who we are before God's face. To acknowledge that we are creatures, that 'it is he that hath made us, and not we ourselves' (Ps. 100.3 [AV]), is to remember that our being is a gift, and therefore we must begin the story we tell about ourselves in our remembering not with ourselves but with God. It is God who 'holdeth our soul in life' (Ps. 66.9 [AV]), and God bestows the gift of personhood on the one who has just been born and on the one whose mind is radically deteriorating as death approaches. This gift does not begin with anything we do, but with God's calling of each person by name. Nor does it end with anything that we do: God, in God's freedom, does not give up on us. We forget God and God's purpose for us, riddling the stories that shape our memory with falsehood and unreality and separating ourselves from truth and life. Yet God does not forget us. It is the divine remembering of us according to God's 'steadfast love' (Ps. 25.7) that sustains the gift of personhood bestowed on us, beyond all human failings and forgetting.

The gift of personhood is therefore itself a promise: the promise of communion with God. It is because God is faithful to that promise that we can recognize human personhood in the stillborn child, the serial killer and the patient in a coma. And it is because of the demonstration of that loving faithfulness in the resurrection of Jesus Christ that we can even name the dead before God as persons, in our prayers and our thanks-giving. When we read the Scriptures, we are not remembering the past as 'another country' separated from us, but recalling human persons who dealt with God and remain our compan-ions today because they remain with us in communion with the one God. Their story – which is also our story – is not fin-ished because God has not finished with them, and therefore we remember. We are, we exist, by the faithfulness of God, a faithfulness that we trace through the witness of Israel and find shining on the face of Christ. That is the story we are continu-ally remembering in the *anamnesis* of public liturgy: the joyful story of who we are before God, because this God is for us and will not abandon us.

To celebrate this good news as we remember together, how-ever, is also to recall how much of ourselves as well as our world remains constrained by the powers of sin and death. We do not therefore need to be hostile to the kind of critique of spiritual optimism that depth psychology can provide. Yet we can also be confident that our personhood begins with God's gift and ends with God's promise, and therefore however great the dis-tance between gift, promise and present actuality, we do not lose hope. Indeed, it is our remembering of the promise that enables us to recognize the distance and make it the matter of our prayer, and to know that such prayer is always heard.

Spiritual formation: meditation

We are formed through continually renewed remembrance that we live by the loving faithfulness of God. We are created persons whose being rests in the gift of communion, not indi-vidual selves who must validate our self-created identities by striving for freedom, knowledge or love set for ever beyond our reach. We remember this by recalling the breadth of all God's works from creation and their depth in the mystery of Christ's cross, together with our own lives in their breadth and depth, with wonder, gratitude and repentance (Ps. 139). Making space for such formation may begin with full participation in the Church's liturgy, including the common hearing of the Scriptures in public worship, but it should not end there. It needs to be extended through some kind of commitment to prayerful reading and study of the Bible. Our practice of such reading then also informs the way we listen to Scripture and scriptural teaching in common worship.

While there have been many different approaches to this through Christian history, one key term for describing what is happening here is 'meditation'. In early monasticism, this tended to mean constant repetition from memory of a particular verse that had struck the monk in the course of the common liturgy.[60] It is worth noting that pre-modern voices regarded memorization as a vital way of internalizing texts, including Scripture. Monks were expected to know the Psalms by heart and recited all 150 at least once every week in the shared worship of Benedictine monasteries. Of course, repetition itself is also a method for seeking to go beyond 'ordinary' consciousness of time and space, from the Jesus prayer and Taizé chanting to contemporary secular dance music.

Subsequent understandings of meditation in the Western Christian tradition show an awareness of the need to create spaces where the recollection of God through Scriptural reading can address the depths of the whole person – including what we might call in modern terminology less conscious dimensions. One increasingly popular form of meditation in the later Middle Ages was to identify with a particular character in

---

60 Jean Leclercq, 1982, *The Love of Learning and the Desire for God: A Study of Monastic Culture*, ET, New York: Fordham University Press, pp. 15–17 and 72–6.

a biblical story and imagine their responses to unfolding events. Devout individuals inside and outside religious orders were taught to enter the stories of the Bible in this way, particularly the Gospels and most particularly of all Jesus' passion. It was a way of remembering these stories as in a very precise sense their stories: stories in which they participated and by which they were shaped. It was another way of recognizing that the 'days of old' from Scripture are also our 'today' (Deut. 32.7; Ps. 77.5).

Terminology and practice alike remained fluid, but some notable attempts were made to define a basic pattern. Perhaps the most famous of these came from a twelfth-century Carthusian called Guigo, who wrote about the 'ladder' of the monk's activity as an ascent from reading to meditation, from meditation to prayer and from prayer to contemplation.[61] For Guigo, meditation is more discursive than imaginative: having read one particular verse or passage, through meditation we recall other verses and passages that might illuminate it. This one text thereby becomes a point of departure for recalling the canon of Scripture as a whole and hence the whole panorama of God's work. Such textual meditation, however, in turn elicits prayer: recalling what God has done from God's fullness, we become mindful of what we lack, of what we are missing. Meditation brings to our consciousness the absence of things we desire: our failures to keep God's commands, our distance from the vision of God. We need the discipline of meditation on Scripture so that these absences can come to our consciousness and we can begin to feel their power. In remembering what God has done, we come to remember how we fall away from our goal, which is communion with God. The trigger for passing from meditation to prayer is the continual remembering of our deepest desire, the desire for God that the Holy Spirit stirs up within us. Prayer

---

61 Simon Tugwell, 1985, *Ways of Imperfection: An Exploration of Christian Spirituality*, Springfield, Illinois: Templegate, pp. 93–124.

is therefore the characteristic action of the person who is truly and deeply aware of their whole self, their whole desire.

Such meditative reading was expected also to raise awareness of our sins and our failings, of our faithlessness before God as well as God's gracious faithfulness. The deliberate remembering of our sins and their articulation in God's presence was also seen as a form of meditation. There is much that could be said here, but what matters for us is that Christians have for many centuries acknowledged that there is deep resistance within us to keeping in mind who we really are before God, and this resistance needs careful and prayerful attention. Sometimes it may mean reviewing the whole of our life up to the present moment and acknowledging how profoundly it is shot through with sinfulness, as in the second exercise of the first week of Ignatius Loyola's *Spiritual Exercises*.[62] It may also mean a regular discipline of preparation to receive communion, or self-examination at the end of each day. This is not because Christians are gloomy people, but because remembering the generosity of God's goodness also makes us mindful of the poverty of our response and the desire for this to be filled with the riches of divine mercy.

Meditation in Christian tradition, therefore, recognizes that there is a need for the long-term undoing and redoing of patterns of memory that exclude the reality of who God is for us and who we are before God. This brings us back to the questions we considered in the previous section about the fracturing of memory. There is an overlap – not an identity – between the remembering of all that we are and have done within meditation as part of spiritual formation, and the opening up of memories that may have been pushed away from consciousness in

---

62 Saint Ignatius of Loyola, 1996, 'The Spiritual Exercises', in *Personal Writings*, ET, London: Penguin, pp. 296–7. For Ignatius' own observance of this practice, see his 'Reminiscences' in the same volume, p. 20.

some forms of counselling and therapy. Where the issues raised in meditation may lead us into the territory of secular therapy, we should not be afraid of following them through its characteristic practices nor of the perspectives and insights that may arise. But it is not a superior form of understanding, and nor is it a substitute. What emerges into the light of reflective memory through therapeutic work needs to be brought into distinctively Christian disciplines of remembrance and offered there: corporate and especially sacramental worship, meditation based on Scripture and the acknowledgement of sin with confidence in God's restoration.

Chapter review

Memory cannot be divorced from meaning: it is through remembering that we make sense of life. Participation in the classic patterns of public liturgy has been fundamental for many centuries in shaping Christians through the formation of Christ-centred memory. Although such participation has been seriously eroded, it remains part of the bedrock of Christian formation and deserves to be creatively sustained. While psychology points towards the scale of our resistance to significant change, this can lead us into a deeper appreciation of human personhood as divine gift and divine promise. Meditation in its various kinds, and in particular meditation on Scripture, has been a crucial practice for opening up the depths of our memory for the work of the Holy Spirit in formation.

8

Understanding

Forming the understanding

Formation for vocation grows through deepening understanding of all that we bring to mind in remembering who God is for us and who we are before God. As we saw in the previous chapter, remembering and understanding are inseparable dimensions of the activity of interpretation that characterizes human persons. We are continually seeking meaning in our experience, by remembering it, asking questions of what we remember and reaching new insights that in turn affect the way we remember what we experience. So it is also with the remembering that forms us in our vocation: it too both depends on and elicits the work of understanding. Psalm 77, for instance, wrestles with the tension between remembering God's mighty works and facing apparent powerlessness here and now. Remembering God as creator and saviour is necessarily theological and invites us to think theologically and to be changed in our understanding. The Spirit who abides in us for ever to form us in responding to the call of Christ is the Spirit of truth, and the Spirit's ministry of keeping Christ in our remembrance is intertwined with the Spirit's ministry of teaching (John 14.17, 26).

Our understanding is formed for a vocation that itself embraces understanding, as noted at the start of Chapter 2 and further explored in Chapter 4. In the beginning, human creatures are given the unique gift of language to make sense in speech of the sense that is always already present in creation, to come to know one another as persons in wonder and love and to work alongside one another in the place that God has set them for the good of the earth. In Christ, we meet the one in whom are all the treasures of knowledge and wisdom, and we are all called, without exception, to grow up into maturity through possessing these riches (Col. 1.24—2.4).

It might seem a relatively easy thing to motivate ourselves and others for growth in understanding in a context where for all the ambivalence about knowledge we discussed in Chapter 2, education and learning are increasingly ubiquitous and indeed celebrated as central for our society. There is challenge as well as opportunity here, however. Education and learning are valued because they enable individuals, organizations and societies to achieve their ends. In the United Kingdom, for instance, policy for Higher Education currently sits within the Department for Business, Innovation and Skills. Lifelong learning might sound appealing, but it also functions as a kind of code for continual training so that we can survive in the jobs we already have and be successful in the jobs we will need to apply for before too long. Learning is necessary for survival and success in the global marketplace, for individuals, corporations and governments, and therefore it is valued. Where a contribution to these things is not evident, learning becomes a kind of leisure pursuit and cannot be considered a serious business.

Such an approach to learning reflects the dominance of the 'common sense' egoism discussed in Chapter 3. Already in the 1940s, it was argued that in popular understanding, 'reasoning' is about finding the best means to ends that are no longer articulated as reasonable for their own sake but justified simply because 'they serve the subject's interest in relation to self-preservation – be it that of the single individual, or of the community on whose maintenance that of the individual depends'.[63] In our own time, we are likely to expect such interest to be expressed in terms that are measurable and quantifiable. And what we are most likely to measure and quantify is money. The value of learning comes down to its price in the market-place, determined by the plausibility of its sales pitch to increase the buyer's resources.[64]

All of this leaves the call to grow in understanding in relation to Christian vocation facing some serious dilemmas. Such growth requires a great deal from us in terms of time, energy, labour and resources, despite the perennial human temptation to think that gaining transformative knowledge can be as simple and instantaneous as pulling an apple off a tree. Can we really afford it, in a late modern society where the Churches are by no means exempt from the perceived economic pressures pushing every organization into the kind of rigorous collective egoism deemed essential for its survival? Is it an investment that can be justified in terms of enhancing output and improving performance? If it cannot, it is bound to struggle to sustain resources, not just finances but allocation of time from those who feel hemmed in by too many demands. And if it can, should we concede that we are giving up on the treasures of Christ's wisdom for the pursuit of what we believe to be more pressing gains?

At this point, I would like to turn again to the Old Testament, and this time to its wisdom literature that overlaps substantially at some points with similar writings from the cultures around it. Wisdom in the Ancient Near East, like education in our present context, was closely associated with power and the skill to achieve results. It is likely that wisdom traditions were honed and passed on partly, though not only, in the context of

---

63 Max Horkheimer, 1974, *Eclipse of Reason*, New York: Continuum, p. 4.

64 Jeremy Carrette, 2007, *Religion and Critical Psychology: Religious Experience in the Knowledge Economy*, Abingdon: Routledge, pp. 61–9.

training for rule and government, from the level of the family and city up to that of the prince and king. The idea that learning wisdom will bring success in social, economic and political activity is evident in the book of Proverbs and in the stories of wise leaders such as Joseph, Solomon and Daniel.

Yet the Old Testament also has some very distinctive things to say about wisdom. To the question, 'But where shall wisdom be found?' (Job 28.12), the answer comes back: 'God understands the way to it, and he knows its place . . . And he said to humankind: "Truly, the fear of the Lord, that is wisdom; and to depart from evil is understanding"' (Job 28.23, 28). In a context where wisdom was readily seen as a means to professional and political advancement, such a statement is jarring. It places a bar against the assumption that wisdom is about me being clever enough to achieve my goals, or the goals set for me by those with power and authority over me. Understanding begins with the end of egoism as the self-justifying pursuit of my self-interest and my concerns. Instead, it means the displacement of self – individual or collective – as the centre and source by acknowledging YHWH as the only God: by faith.

This becomes especially clear in two scriptural narratives where people are described as distinguished by their fear of YHWH.[65] God's declaration that 'now I know that you fear God, since you have not withheld your son, your only son, from me' (Gen. 22.12b) provides a kind of climax to the story of the binding of Isaac and indeed to the narrative of Abraham as a whole. The fear of God means holding on to nothing for myself and putting my whole self, my whole life, my whole future at God's disposal. Abraham thereby becomes a parallel figure to Job, who also endures terrible testing and emerges from it

---

65 R. W. L. Moberley, 2000, *The Bible, Theology, and Faith: A Study of Abraham and Jesus*, Cambridge: Cambridge University Press; David F. Ford, 2007, *Christian Wisdom: Desiring God and Learning in Love*, Cambridge: Cambridge University Press, pp. 90–120.

with divine testimony of constancy in fearing YHWH. In Job's case, this fear is forged through profound questioning and bitter conflict, within himself and with his God, who in the end affirms his wisdom through all his trials. Stripped of all comfort, hope and love, Job does not cease to fear God for nothing – the truth that 'the Satan' can only mock at the start of the drama (Job 1.9). Yet it is only this fear, overlapping with what the New Testament calls faith, that leads to true wisdom: to turning back from evil and towards what is good, true and beautiful. As the epilogue to Job suggests, human flourishing may yet accompany this wisdom. Its aim, however, cannot be our survival and our success, but knowing who God is for us and who we are before God. God's wisdom begins with the renunciation of all egoisms – including those of religious institutions.

Theological formation

'Wisdom cries out in the street; in the squares she raises her voice' (Prov. 1.20). How then do we make space to respond to the call of Christ, the wisdom of God made flesh (1 Cor. 1.24)? Part of the answer here must be about the place of theological formation within Christian formation as a whole. We do not have a choice about doing theology as we respond to God's call. On the other hand, we have choices – many choices – about what kind of theology we do and how we go about it. In this section, I try to establish some basic parameters for how we might make those choices, whether the context is more informal and local or more institutional and educational.

To do this, I would like to distinguish three main senses in which we might use the term 'theology' in the life of the Church.[66]

---

66 I am aware of venturing onto territory that has been extensively covered and slipping into some of the tracks to be found there, e.g. Karl Barth, 1936, *Church Dogmatics* I/1, ET, Edinburgh: T. & T. Clark,

The first sense, which I would call primary theology, is quite simply speaking to and about God, where speaking stands for any kind of activity through which we seek to address God ourselves or communicate God's address to others. Liturgy, sacraments, preaching, prayer, the work of Christian service and witness, art inspired by Christian faith: all of these are primary theology. There is no recognition of God's call, and therefore no vocation, without theology in this sense. In doing primary theology, we respond to our vocation and are formed for it.

As we engage in primary theology, we are bound to become aware both of different perspectives on the meaning of what we say and do from within the life of the Church and of different questions and critiques from outside it. When we dwell on that awareness and seek to explore the issues it raises and articulate our responses, we move into theology in the second major sense I would identify: reflective theology, which reflects on primary theology for the sake of truthfulness in our practice of it. If we would dare to speak to God and about God, then we must take care to test our words against truth, in terms of both what we believe we have heard from God and what we are able to affirm with our hearts and minds, and indeed the tensions between these two. We cannot offer vague or empty words to God or to those who look to us for words to speak about God. Even if we simply repeat words taken from Scripture and tradition, we still need to ask: why have we chosen them and not others, what do we mean by them, how would we explain what we are communicating to someone who asks for help in understanding? The purpose of such investigation, however, is not so that we can accumulate a stock of ideas and arguments, or so that we can gain influence in the Church or in society, but so that what we

pp. 1–11; Aidan Kavanagh, 1984, *On Liturgical Theology*, Collegeville, Minnesota: Liturgical Press; Rowan Williams, 2000, *On Christian Theology*, Oxford: Blackwell, pp. xii–xvi.

say and do in God's name may best correspond to the breadth
and depth of God's Word to us. According to the ancient for-
mula of Evagrius Ponticus, 'If you are a theologian . . . you will
pray truly, and if you pray truly, you are a theologian.'[67]

There is a third sense of theology that we need to bring in at
this point: thinking about God which seeks to bring coherence,
rigour and precision to our reflective theology through extensive engagement with traditions of Christian theology (in all
senses) and with prevalent practices of knowledge within our
culture. This is what people most often mean when they use
the word 'theology', and one reason why it can seem rather off-
putting. Such engagement requires a relatively high level of
general education and a demanding induction into specific academic disciplines, both of which take a great deal of time and
indeed the investment of considerable resources. It is true that
such engagement at first hand is not for everyone within the life
of the Church. But although I have wanted to stress that theology does not begin here and that to participate in the ordinary
things of the Church is to be doing theology, it is also true that
the process we are describing is not a one-way street. Academic
theology (if we can call it that as a short-hand) is almost inevitably accessed by Christians who start to do reflective theology
at any level in the contemporary context, especially given the
instant availability of vast resources deriving more or less
directly from it via the internet. Furthermore, what sense they
make of all this in their reflective theology will then have an
effect on their primary theology – how they hear God's call and
how they begin to respond to it in prayer, worship, service and
witness. These three senses of theology are not closed compart-
ments: they are aspects of a single process that can be usefully
distinguished but not cleanly separated.

---

67 Cited in Vladimir Lossky, 1983, *The Vision of God*, ET, Crestwood, New
York: St Vladimir's Seminary, p. 106.

UNDERSTANDING

Theological formation pivots on the second, reflective sense of theology in particular. Primarily, it is something that we do together in Christian communities that arises from and feeds back into the primary theology expressed in our gathering together as Church and our being sent out as Church into the world. Reflective theology relates particular questions that arise from primary theology to frameworks for understanding faith, of which the historic creeds serve as paradigms. In order to be able to do that, we need to give sustained time, at least at one point in our lives, to learning about such frameworks and thinking through the issues that they raise. This was the purpose of catechesis in the Church of the early centuries – instruction in the faith for those considering baptism – and preparation of young adults for confirmation or church membership in a post-Reformation context. While the latter was generally seen as a matter of memorizing set answers (as set out in 'Catechisms'), the former could take many years, involved examination of attitudes and behaviour as well as formal belief and was followed up in some cases at least by further intensive learning after baptism itself. Arguably, we are now closer to that pre-Christendom Church of the ancient world than to our Victorian predecessors in such matters, and for some decades now there has been a serious attempt to restore a pattern of extended catechesis as fundamental to the theological formation of the whole Church.[68] The widespread use of the Alpha Course from Holy Trinity Brompton perhaps reflects some of the same concerns about establishing a framework of doctrine while also giving space for people to gauge what kind of changes might be involved for them in coming to faith in Christ.

---

68 Maxwell E. Johnson, 1999, *The Rites of Christian Initiation: Their Evolution and Interpretation*, Collegeville, Minnesota: Liturgical Press, pp. 291–363.

133

As well as the need for theological formation of this kind to be considered as an integral and normative part of Christian initiation, however, it is also important for there to be an ongoing commitment to making space for reflective theology within the life of the Christian community. This is partly about nurturing a culture where questions can be articulated, different traditions and perspectives explored and critiques from outside the Church heard without undue defensiveness and hostility. All of this needs to be able to find an appropriate place within the ordinary, ongoing pattern of church life, through both formal, shared activities that are part of an educational programme for all ages and informal conversations and reflections responding to matters as they arise. Inevitably, from time to time this will raise questions about the adequacy of the theological frameworks we learnt to inhabit at formative stages of our own faith journey; there will be a regular if not entirely predictable need to revisit in a more structured and intentional way some of the fundamental issues of Christian belief, and at this point if not before to be clear about the relevance of academic theology. Such theological formation needs to be affirmed not simply with warm words but through a clear commitment to its practice in the face of the twin currents of relentless activism and defensive anxiety that pull powerfully on the life of the contemporary Church at every level.

There are some specific issues here for the theological formation of ordained ministers, who themselves are called to be the primary enablers of such formation for local congregations. With the thorough institutionalization of clergy training over the past two centuries, their theological education is inevitably driven by formal programmes. That does not make their theological formation fundamentally different from what takes place at the level of the local church, however. It will be distinctive in that it will tend to happen as they relate what they are learning through the overt and hidden curricula of such programmes back to primary theology: back to what it means for me with and for others to be addressed by God in worship, prayer and daily life and what it means for me with and for others to respond to the creator of heaven and earth in word and deed. And at that point they too are doing reflective theology but, so to speak, from the other direction than most Christians most of the time, who move from primary theology to reflective theology and only then start to touch on academic theology. If people in training for ministries do not engage in such reflective theology as they undertake the required academic theology, then the accumulation of courses, programmes and degrees, no matter how impressive, will not actually lead to any theological formation at all. This is one reason why older models of formation for ministry in which people did academic theology first and then only later attended to matters practical and spiritual were profoundly flawed, despite their lasting appeal to some constituencies. If we do not begin to learn to do reflective theology out of academic theology when we are actually immersed in it, then it is unlikely we ever will – and unlikely too that we will enrich the theological formation of Christian communities by being able to help them draw constructively on the vast resources of academic theology.

Reflective theology is essential for theological formation, but it can be starved of oxygen by the cultural tendency we identified in the previous section to value knowledge by the results it delivers, where results must serve the needs of an individual or of a collective ego. Reflective theology does not begin with what we want to get, but what we have been given. Indeed, reflective theology means exploring what exactly it is that we want to get, and to what extent it corresponds with the gift of God. As emphasized in Chapter 6, we do not need to get anything more than what has already been given to us in our baptism, while we still yearn to enter into the fullness of that. This is our motivation for seeking to grow in understanding, and for commitment to theological formation for all who are baptized and welcomed among us.

Partial understanding

What I have said in the previous section about the constructive interrelationship between primary, reflective and academic modes of theology expresses my confidence that the rigorous study of theology in an academic context can be and should be enriching for Christian formation. According to a major research project on seminary education in the United States, this is a confidence that is generally shared by the staff of institutions training Christian ministers from across the denominational spectrum, and indeed of those training Jewish rabbis. Yet that same study also found that such staff identified a major 'pedagogical challenge' in enabling students to find a deeper faith through critical thinking about the subject of their faith.[69] The truth is that often students will not share our confidence, and even if they are prepared to engage with open hearts and minds may nonetheless find academic theology arid ground at best for growing in discipleship. We are back with the issue we began to explore at the end of Chapter 2, that the experience of many people in the modern world has been that personal faith and critical thinking do not mix easily and stand in some kind of inevitable tension with, if not contradiction to, each other.

Why should this be the case? If we review the history of Christian theology, we can identify growth in wisdom, in knowing and loving God, as the accepted goal and context for doing theology in quite different periods and traditions prior

---

69 Charles R. Foster, Lisa Dahill, Lawrence A. Golemon and Barbara Wang Tolentino, 2006, *Educating Clergy: Teaching Practices and Pastoral Imagination*, San Francisco: Jossey-Bass, p. 102.

to modernity.[70] It is true that once universities began to be established in the Middle Ages, tensions between the kind of theology that developed there and other traditions of Christian thinking also began to appear.[71] Nonetheless, we might still say that theology was broadly speaking formational in much of pre-modern Christianity: it was about seeking to enable those who acknowledged God's call in Christ to respond more fully, more faithfully and more truthfully to that call. Yet studying academic theology today may appear to have very little to do with Christian formation; indeed, to be a distraction from it. Academic theology seems happy with endless discussion – but the Church needs to make judgements and come to decisions. Academic theology overwhelms us with an impossible variety of disciplines and range of material – but as we could only ever get to grips with a minuscule percentage if we spent our whole lives doing nothing else, why should we even begin? And academic theology requires us to put to one side our deepest convictions and start to evaluate different positions on the basis of reason and argument – but if reason supports conviction, why do we need it, and if reason opposes conviction, where do we go?

If we are to begin to untangle the threads a little here, we need to recognize that they do not relate simply to the formal study of theology. The academic world as a whole can seem like an industry producing overwhelming quantities of material that do not join up with one another or with our lived experience outside it, leaving us at once overfed with information and starved of real wisdom. Beyond that, however, lies the crucial question of what we think we are doing when we seek to grow in knowledge and understanding, and indeed who we think we

---

70 Ellen T. Charry, 1997, *By the Renewing of Your Minds: The Pastoral Function of Christian Doctrine*, Oxford: Oxford University Press.

71 William J. Courtenay, 1987, 'Spirituality and Late Scholasticism', in Jill Raitt (ed.), *Christian Spirituality: High Middle Ages and Reformation*, New York: Crossroad, pp. 109–20.

are when we do this. One place we might look for help here is in the work of Bernard Lonergan, a Canadian Jesuit who wrote on philosophy and theology in the decades after the Second World War. According to Lonergan, in order to participate properly in the human activity of knowing and understanding, we need a particular kind of conversion – what he calls 'intellectual conversion'.

In order to understand what Lonergan means here, we might begin with his description of

> an exceedingly stubborn and misleading myth . . . that knowing is like looking, that objectivity is seeing what is there to be seen and not seeing what is not there, and that the real is what is out there now to be looked at.[72]

Our first inclination, if you like, is to think that knowing is straightforward: the way things are is simply the way they appear to me. Even though adulthood tends to teach us that this is not the case, we are still likely to find ourselves sometimes insisting, 'I just know it', by way of refusing to give any explanation. Our more general reaction to realizing that knowing is not, after all, 'like looking', may be, however, to adopt a new posture of worldly wisdom according to which we cannot really know anything at all: the world is beyond us and therefore inaccessible to us. In philosophical parlance, we move from naïve realism to some form of scepticism, which we also discussed back in Chapter 2. That might sound terribly abstract, but I have observed class discussions where people shift almost seamlessly from one to the other: having initially stated a view as completely obvious to any faithful Christian but finding it challenged, they quickly revert to claiming that since Christians

---

72 Bernard J. F. Lonergan, 1972, *Method in Theology*, London: Darton, Longman & Todd, p. 238.

hold incompatible and irreconcilable views we must simply (and arbitrarily) choose the one that is 'true for us' – and they will choose the one they had in the first place. Although naïve realism and relativist scepticism are diametrical opposites philosophically, what they both have in common is that they make my 'knowledge' impregnable: I cannot come closer to the truth by listening to you, let alone debating with you, so there is no need to try. If we unthinkingly take either of these positions (let alone both), the study of academic theology is indeed pointless.

How are we to move beyond this impasse? Contrary to the myth, Lonergan argues, knowing actually involves working through a process and submitting to a method so that we can really engage with a reality that is indeed beyond us in its totality. It involves discipline and, crucially, collaboration with others, in the present and over time. Human beings are created to grow out of the child's 'world of immediacy' towards the 'world mediated by meaning', which is known only

by the external and internal experience of a cultural community, and by the continuously checked and rechecked judgements of the community. Knowing, accordingly, is not just seeing; it is experiencing, understanding, judging, and believing.[73]

Intellectual conversion, in Lonergan's terms, is about grasping this, sharing in the process of knowing and leaving behind both the myth that 'knowing is like looking' and the reaction against it of sceptical disappointment.

A number of crucial points for Christian formation emerge from Lonergan's analysis here, it seems to me. First, formation in understanding takes time and therefore requires patience. It

73 Lonergan, *Method*, p. 238.

is ultimately a reflection of our solidarity with Adam's fall that we want to be able to snatch at understanding and know everything through an instant of experience. If we are serious about knowing, we will have to work through the cycle of experiencing, then seeking understanding (in the sense of exploring why and how what we have experienced happens the way it does), then formulating judgements about what is true or false from this process of exploration, and finally choosing to believe and act on one or more of those judgements. Nor does this cycle ever arrive at a point where we can stop seeking knowledge because we have somehow 'got it'. Acting on belief generates new experience, needing new understanding and new acts of judging and believing, and so it goes on.

Second, formation in understanding requires an acceptance of our finitude. We can truly 'take part' in knowledge, but we only ever take a part, and our knowledge is always partial. How could it be otherwise if we are finite creatures? If we struggle to accept this, it may be that we still want to be or to make our own god and have not really arrived at that fear of the one creator of heaven and earth which is the true beginning of wisdom. Or it may be that we have not grasped the goodness of the world this God has made and the goodness of time as a cardinal dimension of it. It is a good thing to take time to grow in knowledge and understanding: it is one of the greatest of God's gifts to humankind that we can do this. And it is no hardship that the fullness of knowledge and truth belongs to God and not to us.

Third, formation in understanding requires us to welcome companionship and collaboration. I travel with contemporaries who grapple with the same or related questions and I learn by listening to them and debating with them. I understand only as we understand. This companionship extends into the past too: I start out from points that others have arrived at before me. I understand only from within a tradition, or indeed multiple traditions, received from those who have died. And it even stretches into the future: I pass on my puzzles and my insights to those who come after me. I understand not for my sake only but as a gift to future humanity, so that their 'taking part' in the journey of human knowledge may be richer and fuller. If I resent the fact that knowledge is not something I can ever own and store away as my individual possession, because it is always shared and therefore in that sense too partial, then I betray again the refusal to accept my life as a relational, temporal, embodied creature who lives always from the hand of God.

All of this applies to any kind of sustained human endeavour in seeking understanding: it is relevant for all departments of the university, indeed for all subjects on the school curriculum. It also however has particular relevance for those of us who study academic theology for the sake of reflective theology and therefore for the sake of primary theology, to come back to the terms used in the previous section. It shows how our frustrations about studying theology may well be bound up with the flawed theology of our studying – the implicit theology of human beings, of creation and of the creator that shapes our assumptions here. In particular, it may be that Christians doing theology too often want to compress the four steps in Lonergan's cycle into a single event: we want to pass straight from what we have experienced as Christians to making decisions about what to do as Christians. We should indeed value what we have experienced; approaches to academic theology that tell students their prior experiences in discipleship are irrelevant are both arrogant and ultimately incoherent. Yet we value that experience by opening it up, with proper respect, to critical questioning, by being patient in exploring different perspectives, different explanations, including those that make no appeal to God at all, without rushing to seize on one or the other, indeed allowing that they may be ultimately complementary. Only then can we begin carefully to form a judgement about the matter in hand, and only once we have done that can we shape practical action following from it. In all of this, we should be deeply conscious of our need for God's guidance and our companionship with the communion of saints, while being determined to take our own unique part in the tremendous adventure of human knowledge of divine things. Our understanding will always be partial, but this does not make it valueless; rather, it gives it the value of being both truly human and truly understanding.

Spiritual formation: contemplation

'For now we see in a mirror, dimly, but then we will see face to face. Now I know only in part; then I will know fully, even as I have been fully known' (1 Cor. 13.12). Partial understanding, as discussed in the previous section, belongs to Christian doctrine. Christians should not apologise for knowing 'only in part', nor should they envy those, religious or secular, who claim to possess or to be on the verge of possessing some kind of comprehensive knowledge, for it is only an idol. Yet our partial understanding also has a direction: it is on the way towards fullness, God's fullness. And that fullness will be about knowing not something but someone: our knowing finds its fullness in knowing God, and all persons and all things in God, and God in all persons and all things.

The fullness of human life is knowing God in communion with God: such is the purpose of our calling, one of the persistent themes in Part 2 of this book. Thomas Aquinas, summarizing the teaching of previous centuries, argued that the vision of God is the end for which human beings were created in the beginning and at which they may by God's grace finally arrive: one day we will indeed 'see face to face'. Aquinas also summed up the teaching of earlier theology in the East as well as the West in attributing to every human person a natural desire for God. To be human is to be created to know God and to want to see God with unclouded vision; as Augustine famously expressed it, 'you made us for yourself and our hearts find no peace until they rest in you'.[74] This desire is prone to constant misdirection and is endlessly stifled through foolishness and sin, above all by the tenacious ivy of human idolatry. Yet it is not completely extinguished. In our various desires for peace, for goodness, for love and for knowledge, the desire for God may still stir.

If this is where our knowledge finds its fullness, then our knowledge is inseparable from love: it is only in love that we truly know other human beings, and only in love that we can begin to know God. Of the person seeking God in prayer, William of St Thierry wrote in the twelfth century, 'love itself is understanding for him', a theme that recurs through his writings.[75] For one person to know another there must be a giving and receiving of gifts in love: I must share with you who I am, and you cannot receive this without also sharing who you are with me. Yet the teaching of pre-modern Christianity was that while we have a natural desire to know God, we have no natural power to achieve this. As creatures, we have no means to share God's being, to be in loving communion with God and in such communion to know God. Human persons are therefore unique within all creation. To paraphrase Aquinas' teaching on this point, 'Only human nature finds its perfection *beyond* itself; it dynamically tends to a goal that it is incapable of attaining by its own powers.'[76] We find the same doctrine in

---

74 Saint Augustine, 1961, *Confessions*, ET, Harmondsworth: Penguin, p. 21 (I.1).

75 William of St Thierry, 1971, *The Golden Epistle: A Letter to the Brethren at Mont Dieu*, ET, Kalamazoo, Michigan: Cistercian Publications, p. 68. For some contemporary reflections on this theme, see Oliver O'Donovan, 2002, *Common Objects of Love: Moral Reflection and the Shaping of Community*, Grand Rapids, Michigan: Eerdmans, pp. 9–16.

76 Louis Dupré, Henri de Lubac, 2000, *Augustinianism and Modern Theology*, Lancelot Sheppard, New York: Crossroad, p. xiv.

Richard Hooker: the eternal delight in God which alone can satisfy the human soul

> . . . doth neither depend upon the nature of the thing itself, nor proceed from any natural necessity that our souls should so exercise themselves forever in beholding and loving God, but from the will of God, which doth both freely perfect our nature in so high a degree, and continue it so perfected.[77]

Only by God's free grace can our nature reach the end for which it always longs.

The fullness of our knowledge, then, the knowledge of God for which we are always thirsting, is something that we can only receive from God as a gift, as sheer grace. And in order to receive it, we must let go of the knowledge we have achieved without this grace. Everything we can possibly think about God, even when our thinking uses words from Scripture, is shaped by our experience of created reality and is therefore bound to misrepresent the creator in a radical way. This insight has led to the cultivation of the 'way of negation' in Christian theology and spirituality: even our truest thoughts about God and the statements we use to express them must be negated, as it were crossed out even though we let them remain legible because we know they are still saying something of the greatest importance. Here too, the renewal of our creation's promise of communion with God is inseparable from following the crucified Christ. Entering into the face-to-face knowledge of God means learning how utterly radical is our need to leave behind everything we know, in order for a true response to God's call to be sustained by our whole being in union with Christ the risen Lord.[78]

---

77 Richard Hooker, 1907, *Of the Laws of Ecclesiastical Polity: Books 1 to 4*, London: Dent, p. 204 (I.XI.3).

78 Edith Stein, 2002, *The Science of the Cross*, ET, Washington DC: ICS Publications.

Christian tradition teaches that while the fullness of this knowledge belongs with the resurrection of the dead and the life of the world to come, it is possible to receive glimpses of it here and now. One significant term within the tradition here is 'contemplation', and indeed there has been something of a revival of Christian contemplative prayer since the 1960s.[79] Western medieval writers taught that such contemplation, in silence full of love, could and properly should follow from profound meditation on Scripture. Recalling what God has done with words, ideas, stories and imagination grounds us in the knowledge of God and of ourselves, but it also keeps bringing us to the limits of our capacity to comprehend who this God is who has so graciously met us in creation, revelation and redemption. As Guigo II develops these themes in the work referred to at the end of the previous chapter, reading Scripture takes us into meditation arising from Scripture, which takes us into prayer for the fullness of the gift we hear of in the Scripture, which then takes us into a waiting on God to receive this gift more fully. Because the gift is communion with the infinite God, contemplation becomes the door that opens into it.

It would be wrong to think of contemplation as something that takes us away from other people and from the world. It may be that there is a kind of 'training' of our vision that requires us to step aside from the thoughts and activities that habitually crowd our minds. Solitude and silence are likely to be part of that, and we should value the space they open up, not run away from it. A glimpse of God, however, is a glimpse of the creator of heaven and earth, and this must change the way we see and know the things of heaven and earth. A glimpse of God is a glimpse of the one who loved the world so much that he gave his only Son for the life of humanity, and this must change the

---

79 See, e.g., Thomas Merton, 1973, *Contemplative Prayer*, London: Darton, Longman & Todd.

way we see humanity. We cannot know this God without love, and we cannot love this God without loving what God loves and seeking what God seeks. Contemplation and action, knowing and serving, are held together inseparably in love.

We will return to this theme in the next chapter, but first it is perhaps worth returning to the beginning of this one where we noted the contemporary tendency to value knowledge as a way for me to secure and advance my interests. In the light of what we have said through the chapter as a whole, Christian formation must lead us away from this towards a practice of knowing that always has a contemplative dimension. Whatever we are seeking to understand, we will know it best with an attentive and loving gaze that recognizes the work of the infinite creator and, in the case of human persons, the presence of the divine image. Gregory of Nyssa, one of the first Christian thinkers to speak openly of God's incomprehensibility, also argued that one of the ways in which human beings reflect God's image is by 'figuring by its own unknowableness the incomprehensible Nature' of God.[80] Just as there is no end to knowing and loving God, there is no end to knowing and loving any human person.

Chapter review

Society encourages us to gain understanding where it relates to some project sanctioned by individual or collective egoism. Christian commitment to theological formation – in the local congregation as well as the seminary or college – needs to come instead from thankfulness for the mystery of our salvation and the desire to know it more fully. Such theological formation pivots on the role of 'reflective theology' in making space for

---

80 Gregory of Nyssa, 1892, *On the Making of Man*, XI.4, text from www.ccel.org/ccel/schaff/npnf205.x.ii.ii.xii.html.

faithful conversation about the truth of what we say and do in Christ's name. Reflective theology is nourished by academic theology, yet academic knowledge can appear at once overwhelming and irrelevant. Responding to the challenges here involves thinking about how we come to know truth as human creatures. It also draws us towards the practice of contemplation as understanding that gazes on the face of the creator who always exceeds our understanding.

9

Willing

Forming the will

In responding to God's call, it is our will that accepts or resists, or indeed accepts in part and resists in part. It is therefore crucial that our will is being formed if we are to be shaped by and for our vocation. 'Will' may sound a rather old-fashioned word when not preceded by 'free', and I would hope that Chapter 1 might have helped us to see why this should be so. Our willing is that which directs and drives our lives, but modernity makes it difficult for us to imagine a directing that could be truly ours that does not consist in successive acts of individual and independent choice.

In the context of the theological understanding set out in Part 2 of this book, it should be evident that for Christians also the freedom of the human will is of great importance and to be resolutely defended against the constant threat of determinism in its various forms. Yet for Christian theology, this freedom is found first and foremost in responding to God's word, God's free act: it is about accepting the gift of the creator, not striving to become the creators of ourselves. Only such acceptance can release the creativity that belongs to us as creatures made in the image of the creator; only service of the God who saves us can liberate us from sin and the shadows of sin for life, life in its extraordinary fullness.

How then is our will formed for the purpose of our calling, which we summed up in Chapter 6 as becoming conformed to the eternal Son of God through renewal of the image in which we were created, participation in God's eternal life and following Jesus day by day? The answer in every case takes us back to the same place: love. As with freedom, we need to recognize that theology must hold together what modernity has tended to put asunder. Love is delight and discipline, ecstasy and commitment. To pick up the discussion at the end of the previous chapter, it encompasses both contemplation and action, gazing on the face of the beloved and determination to do love's work. In this final chapter, the focus is on how our will is formed in order for us to say yes ever more fully to the call of God and hence inhabit ever more deeply the freedom of the glory of the children of God (Rom. 8.21). And the formation of our will takes place in love.

What kind of love is it, then, that should fill the willing that directs us day by day? Different passages from the New Testament express it in different though complementary ways. The basic unanimity of diverse texts on the centrality of love derives from the teaching of Jesus himself, as evidenced in the passages about his discussion of priority within the commandments given to Israel at Sinai:

> 'You shall love the Lord your God with all your heart, and with all your soul, and with all your mind.' This is the greatest and first commandment. And a second is like it: 'You shall love your neighbour as yourself.' On these two commandments hang all the law and the prophets. (Matt. 22.37–40)

As suggested in Chapter 7 with regard to the Ten Commandments, we cannot hear God's guidance on how to act aside from remembering God's revelation about who God is; each must be interpreted in the light of the other. So too in the teaching of Jesus: the call to love God and to love the neighbour without limits is inseparable from the demonstration in Jesus of the love of God for the world without limits. To follow in his footsteps is to walk the way of love. To recognize in him the eternal Son of God is to know the truth that God is love and that only by participating in that love can we find the gracious fulfilment of our humanity. To say that he is the image of the invisible God in which we were created is to know that image in the crucified Christ, the one who emptied himself for us and our salvation. In God's search for our human love, which we trace in the story of Israel and the person of Christ, we begin to glimpse the unfathomable depths of God's love for us. All the commandments are given so that we may show our love of the one who calls us and thereby recognize in them the call of the lover to be loved by us.[81] As already stressed, love as committed action leads to love as joyful contemplation, and love as gift received by grace leads back to love as gifts offered in joyful service.

Indeed, Scripture teaches that the love we have for God is itself the gift of God; that in our free choosing to act for the love of God, God is always at work. The prophets Jeremiah and Ezekiel both speak of God acting on the hearts of God's people so that the covenant and its commands might be kept after so many failings (Jer. 31.31–34; Ezek. 11.19–20; 36.26–27). In Romans, Paul affirms that 'God's love has been poured into our hearts through the Holy Spirit that has been given to us' (Rom. 5.5). In Galatians, love is the first fruit of the Holy Spirit – indeed, given that Paul speaks about the fruit of the Spirit in the singular here, we might see love as the primary fruit that then grows a series of distinctive traits in those who belong to Christ and have been crucified with him (Gal. 5.22–24). The love by which we love God, enabling our natural desire for God to approach its true object, is the gift of God the Holy Spirit.

---

81 Franz Rosenzweig, 2005, *The Star of Redemption*, ET, Madison, Wisconsin: University of Wisconsin Press, pp. 190–2.

As has been emphasized in the rest of Part 3, the work of the Holy Spirit in our formation does not mean there is no work for us to do. The New Testament, like the Old, is full of specific instructions about how the command to love is to be lived in practice. Jesus gives his disciples commands (Matt. 28.20); Paul does the same for his readers, sometimes distinguishing carefully the status of the rulings he hands down (e.g. 1 Cor. 7.10–12). Moreover, such teaching is interwoven with descriptions of the qualities of character that Christians should intentionally foster as they follow such instruction. Paul did not see a tension between describing as fruits of the Spirit traits that he can elsewhere instruct his readers to practise in their daily behaviour: love, joy, peace and patience all reappear in his brisk guidance on community living in Romans 12, for instance, and love, peace, patience, kindness and gentleness in what he has to say to the Colossians at 3.12–17.

Such lists of traits of character have an important role in connecting the centrality of the single commandment to love with the multifaceted experience of following Jesus day by day. Love has a primary and pivotal place within these lists, but it is also articulated in terms of other qualities, or perhaps better, dispositions. We do not simply want to conform in terms of our outward behaviour to what is right in God's sight: we want to want what God wants, to become the kind of people who do the will of God because their wills are patterned according to God's ways. This means nurturing specific dispositions, such as joy, patience and kindness, by dwelling on what is true, honourable, just, pure, pleasing and commendable, and on 'excellence' (Phil. 4.8) – a Greek word normally translated elsewhere in similar contexts as 'virtue'.

Virtue was a familiar concept in the ancient world. The Greek term did indeed have 'excellence' as its basic meaning: a virtuous life was a life of human excellence, a life lived well. And such a life would be characterized by particular excellences, particular virtues: habits of thinking and acting that together constituted what a good human life should be like. Although the word itself is rare in the New Testament, Christian tradition soon adopted the language of virtue and the virtues to articulate scriptural teaching about the formation of the will for love through the fostering of what we have been calling traits, dispositions or qualities of character.[82] For Augustine, for instance, virtue is the *ordo amoris*, the ordering of love. In his great thirteenth-century synthesis for university theology students, Thomas Aquinas drew on Paul's triad of faith, hope and love to develop Christian teaching about the theological virtues. In the same century but in the very different context of the emerging Beguine communities, Hadewijch could write in one of her letters about the dangers of prioritizing 'sweetness' – ecstatic experience linked to the practice of contemplation we were describing at the end of the previous chapter – over the virtues in seeking to grow in the love of God:

> Virtues and not sweetness are the proof of love, for it sometimes happens that he who loves less feels more sweetness. Love is not in each person according to what he feels, but according as he is *grounded* in virtue *and rooted in charity* (Eph. 3.17).[83]

Moral formation

On the basis of what we have said over the previous two chapters, moral formation, liturgical formation and theological

---

82 On virtue in the New Testament, see Tom Wright, 2010, *Virtue Reborn*, London: SPCK.

83 Hadewijch, 1980, *The Complete Works*, ET, New York: Paulist Press, p. 66 (italics in original).

formation are interwoven. Liturgical formation is where we learn what it means to live as God's companions, where we both model and practise the virtues that constitute the pattern of Christian life.[84] Theological formation includes reflection about what we should *do* in the name of Christ as an integral part of our whole 'speaking' to and about God. Liturgical and theological formation flow into moral formation, as the formation of the will to do what is good and right. Moreover, without such willing on our part, the discipline and indeed the right motivation needed for liturgical and theological formation will inevitably be lacking.

There is, then, no Christian formation which does not include moral formation as an integral dimension. As Hadewijch stressed in the thirteenth century, earnest spiritual searching that wants to float free of constant grounding in the work of moral formation is always dangerous. Flaws and failings in the moral formation of individual Christians, especially Christian leaders, and indeed whole communities and institutions can be tragically destructive for the well-being of the body of Christ and for witness to Christ before the world. There is simply no way to grow in the love by which alone we can reach the purpose of our calling without the training of our will in moral formation. Why, then, is moral formation perhaps harder to talk about directly than spiritual, liturgical or theological formation? Why is it less likely to attract any kind of formal or indeed informal assessment in the context of ministerial formation? And why might clergy today feel rather reticent about dealing with what was quite simply the bread and butter of their predecessors' activity for much of the past two millennia?

One possible answer is that we have become estranged from the tradition of the virtues that underpinned constructive thinking

---

84 Samuel Wells, 2006, *God's Companions: Reimagining Christian Ethics*, Malden, Massachusetts: Blackwell.

about moral formation, both theoretical and practical, for our forebears. In one of the most influential books of philosophy published in the past half-century, Alasdair MacIntyre traced this tradition from the ancient Greeks, through its adoption and revision by Christian thinkers from the New Testament onwards and into the modern world. Here, he argued, it becomes desperately obscured, leaving us in a society 'after virtue' (the title of his book) and therefore devoid of any integrating under-standing of moral life.[85]

It might be useful at this point to offer a brief sketch of how that long tradition viewed moral formation by briefly consid-ering the 'cardinal virtues' identified by medieval writers from their reading of the classical tradition: temperance, courage, prudence and justice.[86] We are unlikely to hear many sermons on temperance today, though Paul has plenty to say about it to Titus (Titus 1.8; 2.2, 2.5, 2.6, 2.12). To exercise moral will at any level, however, we have to learn to say: 'I recognize that my desire is to do X – and I am not going to do X immediately.' That is to begin to practise the virtue of temperance, of not being ruled by my immediate desires and instincts. There is no moral living without some detachment of this sort; without becoming someone who *has* desires (and can therefore question them and interrupt them) rather than someone who simply *is* their de-sires, is constituted by them.

We can make similar points about the remaining three card-inal virtues as well. To become capable of sustaining moral action, for instance, we have to learn how to say: 'I believe X is the right thing for me to do, and even though I risk painful consequences if I choose it, I will do it regardless.' That is to begin to exercise the virtue of courage. There is no overall human

---

85 Alasdair MacIntyre, 1985, *After Virtue: A Study in Moral Theory*, 2nd edn, London: Duckworth.

86 Alasdair MacIntyre, 2009, *Dependent Rational Animals: Why Human Beings Need the Virtues*, rev. edn, London: Duckworth, pp. 81–98.

excellence, we might say, in the life of people or indeed organizations that constantly worry about 'covering their own backs' as the primary issue; that is because they are deficient in the specific excellence of courage. Then again, to live as moral beings, we have to learn how to come to a decision when different good things appear to be in conflict, for instance when doing what I believe to be right risks painful consequences not just for me but for others too for whom I have a responsibility. And that kind of ability to weigh up issues in moral deliberation is what the ancient Greeks meant by prudence. This too is fundamental for moral formation. Finally, the virtue of justice might be expressed in terms of commitment to what is right and fair as an obligation under which I place myself and thereby refuse to treat myself as some kind of exception to the rules and norms that apply to others. We cannot sustain a moral life without that either. No wonder that these four, temperance, courage, prudence and justice, came to be referred to as the cardinal virtues, 'cardinal' coming from the Latin word for hinge – the virtues on which all the rest hinge, all the rest turn.

How do we learn these virtues? The traditional answer would be in a way that is analogous to how we learn practical skills and become good at doing things in other areas. To achieve excellence in athletics or music, we take it for granted that attention to those who are already skilled, constant and even repetitive practice and willingness to accept and learn from direct supervision are all necessary. So it is also with the excellences we call the virtues, the excellences of human life as a whole. We begin to acquire them by observing others who already possess them, submitting to their authority and trying to follow their guidance for ourselves alongside others. We need examples, mentors and companions: we need a community. We work at practising these excellences until they become deeply engrained habits of thinking and behaving, which means a commitment that can survive distraction when other things seem more interesting or attractive. Hence Paul can say to the Philippians, 'Keep on doing the things that you have learned and received and heard and seen in me, and the God of peace will be with you' (Phil. 4.9).

The early Christians transformed the ancient tradition of the virtues by transposing it to life in Christ. The Church now becomes the primary context for moral formation. Our will is shaped by and for the love of God as we learn through practices keyed to the sacraments of baptism and Eucharist what it means to live every day resurrection from the dead as the one true story of human fulfilment. The gathering of the body of Christ crucified and risen has to overflow into changed wills and therefore changed lives: 'And let us consider how to provoke one another to love and good deeds, not neglecting to meet together, as is the habit of some, but encouraging one another, and all the more as you see the Day approaching' (Heb. 10.24–25). Meeting together in the name of Christ results in mutual provocation to love, expressed in good deeds and in the growth of traits of character that produce good deeds as a tree produces its fruit. Paul tells Titus that Christ's desire is that we should be 'a people of his own who are zealous for good deeds' (Titus 2.14). As we remember what God has done in divine love more completely and understand it more deeply, so we should love God and one another more fully by practising those virtues that enable God's love to flow through us and find its home among us.

If we are to take moral formation seriously in Christian communities and institutions today, we need to affirm that the shaping of the will for love through the practice of the virtues is necessary, difficult and possible. It is necessary, although the expressive individualism of our culture finds it incomprehensible: because our only duty on this account is to be true to our individual selves, without getting in the way of other individual selves doing likewise. Where such thinking has influence, moral formation is unlikely to find much purchase. It is also, however, difficult, as we will consider more fully in the next section, and therefore simply lecturing people about rules they must follow will produce little fruit beyond either complacency or guilt, which may then seek relief in the adoption of the very moral relativism that the person laying down the rules is seeking to oppose. While specific guidance has a necessary place in moral formation, the good news is not that there are rules we can follow but that there is grace through which we can come to love what God loves with our whole heart. And it is possible because grace is real, because God speaks and acts, not because we have any capacity to grow in goodness independently from the action of God. We find confidence in its possibility not by looking to ourselves and our achievements but by attending to the reflection of Christ's likeness in the Church, beginning with those persons in whom it is especially visible, whom some would call saints.

Preachers and teachers at every level of the Church have a clear responsibility to nurture such moral formation. In what became one of the great classics of the medieval world, Gregory the Great presented the task of those who hold responsibility in the Church as drawing people towards the vision of God by strengthening them in the virtues through preaching , by which he clearly means something much broader than formal preaching in the context of worship.[87] For him, the virtues are what 'settle' our lives into an order, a pattern, that frees us to know God, to love God and finally to see God. A key task for preachers is therefore to make an assessment of the people in front of them in terms of which virtues they especially need in order to love God more in their specific circumstances – and to know how to commend them and make them attractive.

---

87 Saint Gregory the Great, 1950, *Pastoral Care*, ET, Westminster, Maryland: Newman Press.

Christian communities of all kinds should be places of virtuous conversation, where we 'consider how to provoke one another to love and good deeds'. Such shared conversation should grow from and feed into more personal reflection. Each of us needs to give some time to asking prayerfully and carefully where we have been able to grow in the virtues that form our wills for the love of God, where we have failed in the expression of those virtues and where we need to seek strengthening in a particular virtue in order to be faithful to Christ where we are. This might be done each day as part of a review before God, or once a week as part of preparation for sharing in the worship of the Lord's people on the Lord's day. For some, the discipline of naming our failures out loud to another person and seeking with them God's transforming grace may also be important, whether described in terms of the sacrament of reconciliation in Catholic contexts or a more literal adherence to the advice of James 5.16.

Divided will

If we take seriously the challenge of moral formation, sooner or later we are likely to find ourselves at an impasse. It might be that a virtue that we think we can ordinarily show in our dealings with others – say, compassion – seems completely inaccessible when we are faced with the suffering of a specific individual. Or perhaps we are aware that one of the fruits of the Spirit seems strangely reluctant to grow in our case, despite our best efforts to practise it and our prayers for God's grace to nurture it. Or we may become suddenly conscious of what seems to be a serious flaw in our moral character, as a result of a casual remark, an overheard conversation or even an explosive confrontation. While we have believed we are really willing the transformation of our will by and for God's love, something seems to have got stuck, and our actual will seems stubbornly resistant to any change.

Perhaps the first thing to say is that we should not be surprised when this happens. Already in the letter to the Romans, Paul devotes an extended passage to the tension which characterizes his own experience as well as illuminating the human condition.[88] As he sums matters up:

> So I find it to be a law that when I want to do what is good, evil lies close at hand. For I delight in the law of God in my inmost self, but I see in my members another law at war with the law of my mind, making me captive to the law of sin that dwells in my members. (Rom. 7.21–23)

We might compare this with Augustine's famous account (written many years after the event) in *Confessions* Book VIII of his conversion to Christian faith. Augustine vividly portrays the conflicting desires at work within him, pulling him now towards, now away from God's will as the balance of internal powers constantly shifts. 'My inner self was a house divided against itself', he writes.[89] Augustine was also clear that while conversion leads to a new beginning and life is transformed by faith that leads to love, the struggle never leaves us. There is always that within us which resists and drags against the work of grace, sending us back to old ways.

Augustine analysed this continual division within the human will in terms of conflicting loves. The will is always loving something: loving is what the will does. Fallen humanity, however, is dominated by love of things in the world, which is itself ultimately an expression of love of self: we make ourselves

---

88 Cf. James D. G. Dunne, 1988, *Romans 1—8*, Word Biblical Commentary 38a, Dallas, Texas: Word Books, pp. 399–412.

89 Saint Augustine, 1961, *Confessions*, ET, Harmondsworth: Penguin, p. 170 (VIII.8).

the final object of our own desiring, blocking out the desire for God that is at the root of our true humanity according to the teaching we considered at the end of the previous chapter. For Augustine, even when we think we are acting for the sake of others or just doing our duty, self-love is always at work and by its presence rendering all our actions sinful. The gift of the love of God does truly release us from the endlessly repeating loops of self-love and liberate us to love others. Yet though by faith we receive this gift through the pouring out of God's Holy Spirit in our hearts, self-love does not evaporate but remains to struggle with love for God and for our neighbour for as long as we live on this earth. To be human is to love, yet love of different things is always pulling us in more than one direction.

So what are we to do when we feel this tug of contrary loves dividing our will? Traditional advice has tended to recommend increased spiritual activity: more commitment to individual and shared intercession, fuller participation in the Church's worship and sacraments, greater self-discipline and conscious renunciation of distracting attachments. Nor is any of this bad advice as such, though certainly care needs to be taken as to how it is given and how it is received. Yet at one point or another, it may not seem to take us very far and leave us in danger of moving from frustration to disillusionment.

One way to try to understand what is happening would be to see it in the light of the premise of depth psychology as discussed in Chapter 7: the pervasiveness of a conscious–unconscious dynamic in human selfhood. To begin with, we might then perceive that our frustrations here are at some level about a struggle to acknowledge reality. Our conscious mind that thinks, plans, organizes and pursues goals is not the whole truth about who we are. It is not an illusion or a mistake, but neither is it the whole story. We are not free to be whatever we want to be, as the late modern secular gospel preaches. We are creatures in time, profoundly conditioned by our own deepest past from which we are not able to walk away as if we can decide in the present moment on the person we will become. We cannot autonomously choose the goals we will give our lives to pursuing, because even in such high-minded moments we are constantly pushed and pulled by desires of which we are at best only dimly aware. There is a profound continuity between Freudian and Augustinian insights here, converging against the constant illusion of self-mastery as the hallmark of the modern self.[90]

All of this might teach us to have more patience with both ourselves and others in seeking the formation of our wills through their integration in divine love. It might also make us more alert to moments when fragments of our willing that are normally hidden unexpectedly break through the surface and into our consciousness. However alarming and even distressing such occasions may be, we can see them as opening up more truth about ourselves and therefore enabling us to offer up more of ourselves to the light of Christ. When we find ourselves suddenly, overwhelmingly and apparently unaccountably angry, sad or joyful, viscerally attached to another person or hostile to another person, it is worth pondering the question: is something about me revealing itself here whose power is usually hidden?

The work of the Institute of Psychology of the Gregorian University in Rome indicates the potentially critical importance of such moments for Christian formation. Its founder members set up a large-scale research project in the 1970s to follow various groups of young American Roman Catholics who were seeking to fulfil some kind of vocation (to the priesthood, the religious life or to teaching in Catholic schools).[91] Their central hypothesis was that vocational consistency is a

---

90 Iris Murdoch, 1970, *The Sovereignty of Good*, London: Routledge & Kegan Paul, pp. 50–2.

91 L. M. Rulla, F. Imoda and J. Ridick, 1988, *Psychological Structure and Vocation*, Rome: Gregorian University Press.

major indicator of vocational flourishing in Christian ministry. Vocational consistency here is about the 'fit' between what people believe the Church expects from its ministers, what they aspire to for themselves in ministry, what they actually know about themselves and what they do not know about themselves but remains operative unconsciously. It is not that all these should be identical (how could they?), but that there should be a relatively creative tension between them and a reasonable degree of convergence. The conclusion of the research seemed to bear out strongly this initial hypothesis. 'Central inconsistencies' between strong, unconscious needs on the one hand and conscious ideals and values on the other, noted at an early stage of education and training, were an effective predictor for not sustaining or never even beginning the chosen vocational role. Perhaps more surprisingly, the research also suggested that six years in a highly focused and all-absorbing seminary environment actually seemed to have little or no effect on a person's vocational consistency, or indeed general psychological maturity. Much of the work of the Institute since then has been about developing more effective approaches to formation in the context of priesthood and the religious life.[92]

One of its leading figures argued that the crux of the problem for most people in formation for vocation comes from specific areas of entanglement between 'conscious and unconscious structures'.[93] My consciously held motivations in seeking to respond to the call of God interact negatively in this case with less conscious motivations that either keep skewing the way I respond in a particular direction so as to meet some unconscious need at the same time, or act as a kind of mental handbrake that

92 Franco Imoda, ed., 2000, *A Journey to Freedom: An Interdisciplinary Approach to the Anthropology of Formation*, Studies in Spirituality Supplement 5, Leuven: Peeters.

93 L. M. Rulla, 1986, *Anthropology of the Christian Vocation*, Vol. I: *Interdisciplinary Bases*, Rome: Gregorian University Press, p. 180.

diminishes my response with ambivalence if not resentment at needs denied. For instance, I may genuinely believe that preaching is at the heart of my calling and vital for the well-being of the Church, but I may also be drawn to opportunities to stand at the centre of the attention of others and reveal to them aspects of myself. That is not necessarily wrong or problematic, but if I have no awareness of it (or some awareness that I find it very difficult to acknowledge), I may end up preaching in ways that are more about satisfying my unrecognized emotional needs than actually feeding the congregation with sound teaching. Moreover, I may find myself prioritizing sermon preparation to the exclusion of other aspects of my calling and justifying such neglect on the grounds of serving others, unable to acknowledge that I am actually indulging myself. I may also start to wonder why I have no real interest in aspects of ministry whose common denominator is that they are not clearly visible to others and attract no attention, such as routine administration or private prayer.

There is a great deal more that could be said here, but I hope this is enough to show the crucial importance in Christian formation of acknowledging the reality of our divided will and being prepared to take notice of the deeper underlying conflicts that may sometimes float to the surface. These are moments of great opportunity for grace, as well as potential danger for sin. For that opportunity to be taken, having someone who will listen to us with patience and speak to us with wisdom is likely to be vital. That is one reason why cultivating and being committed to such relationships is a basic duty for us if our will really is to be formed for our vocation. Different language will be used in different Christian traditions, from spiritual direction to mentoring and accountability; for some, it will seem obvious that such relationships are properly mutual, while for others that would undercut their value; the place of psychological insight and therapeutic skills will be critical for some but seem irrelevant to others. Whatever we make of these issues, we need to pray for relationships of patient listening and wise speaking and treasure them where we find them.

Spiritual formation: election

In the previous section, we were reflecting on the experience of willing what is good and yet finding ourselves drawn back to what is bad or less good. What about situations, however, where we are faced with two or more things that are both basically good? How is our willing formed by God's love in such contexts – or is it just down to us to make the call?

The question is particularly significant for the distinctive vocations that we discussed in the final two sections of Chapter 6. Decisions about whether to become a midwife or an engineer, whether to seek marriage or remain single, whether to offer myself for ordained ministry or continue to serve God as I am now – these are not moral choices in the sense of choices between good things and bad things or even between one thing that is obviously better and another that is clearly worse. Such decisions are rarely made instantaneously, but there are still critical moments when we are aware of the magnitude of going forward and the magnitude likewise of staying put. Moreover, the larger choices, such as profession, marriage and ordination, once settled open up a continuing series of further choices following from them that has no definite end: when to seek a major enhancement of responsibility, where to bring up a family, whether to remain in the ministerial office that I currently hold.

The classic discussion of how we should approach such vocational discernment occurs in the *Spiritual Exercises* of Ignatius Loyola, in material placed at the end of the second week.[94]

---

94 Saint Ignatius of Loyola, 1996, 'Spiritual Exercises', in *Personal Writings*, ET, London: Penguin, pp. 316–20.

Ignatius lists three times, or occasions, for making what he calls an 'election', i.e. a conscious choice about commitments that will decisively shape the way we live out our vocation. The first, he writes, is 'when God Our Lord so moves and attracts the will that without doubting or being able to doubt, such a dedicated soul follows what is shown, just as St Paul and St Matthew did when they followed Christ our Lord'.[95] He does not rule out the possibility of our being immediately clear and confident about the choice we should make as a result of God's speaking to us through how God 'moves the will'; indeed, he seems to have assumed that this would happen for some people undertaking the exercises.[96]

Much more attention is given, however, to the second and third times for making an election. The second might arise from the practices of meditation and contemplation as we have described them in the past two chapters, although it is not restricted to this: 'when sufficient light and knowledge is received through experience of consolations and desolations, and through experience of the discernment of different spirits'.[97] Although little more is said at this point, these are terms that recur frequently throughout the *Exercises* and to which Ignatius devotes two lengthy sets of 'Rules' later on. Consolations are feelings of joy and peace that flow from adhering to the will of God, and desolations are feelings of 'darkness and disturbance in the soul' that come from the influence of powers hostile to God in our soul.[98] Attending to their shifting tides as we consider different possibilities for living out our vocation can be a significant way in which God guides us in our choices. Yet it is not always easy to recognize which is really which – hence

---

95 Ignatius, 'Spiritual Exercises', p. 317.

96 Harvey D. Egan, 1987, *Ignatius Loyola the Mystic*, Wilmington, Delaware: Michael Glazier, pp. 150–1.

97 Ignatius, 'Spiritual Exercises', p. 317.

98 Ignatius, 'Spiritual Exercises', pp. 348–53.

the vital importance of 'discernment of spirits' both for self-understanding and for making vocational choices when these seem to arise out of our spiritual activities.

The third time for making an election is described as a time of quiet:

> One considers first of all the purpose for which human beings exist, viz. to praise God Our Lord and to save their souls. Desiring this end, one chooses as means some life or state within the limits set by the Church, in order to find thereby a help to the service of one's Lord and the salvation of one's soul.[99]

Ignatius has much more to say about this than either of the first two at this point in the *Exercises*. He outlines two ways of approaching this 'third time', the second of which consists mainly in a series of imaginative exercises whereby we imagine how different outcomes to our choosing might appear in another context – advising a stranger in the same situation, facing our own death or appearing before Christ in judgement. The first involves a series of steps, all hinging on maintaining a complete focus on 'the end for which I was created, viz. to praise God Our Lord and save my soul'.[100] In the light of what we have said in Chapter 6 in particular, we might want to express this somewhat differently in terms of becoming more fully conformed to the image of God's Son in relation to the scriptural themes of creation, communion and discipleship. Yet Ignatius is surely right to insist that only by focusing very clearly on the purpose of our calling can we hope to think and pray rigorously about how we are to live out that calling in relation to concrete decisions. In order to do this, he advises us to make a structured

---

99 Ignatius, 'Spiritual Exercises', pp. 317–18.
100 Ignatius, 'Spiritual Exercises', p. 318.

analysis of the possibilities before us. First, we list the 'advantages or benefits' in relation to fulfilling the purpose of our calling from seeking this new thing. Second, we list the things that may constitute 'disadvantages and dangers' in the same light. We then repeat the exercise, but this time in relation to not seeking what we are considering: what are the 'advantages and benefits' here, and what are the 'disadvantages and dangers', always in relation to our end, our purpose?[101]

One of the great privileges of working in ministerial formation is that I hear many people's stories about how they have come to believe they have a vocation to ordained ministry. I can recognize variations on all three of the 'times' of election Ignatius describes. The first two relate to a pattern in which vocation is felt to begin from within the person's own spiritual life, either very dramatically (the first time), or more slowly and sometimes only over a number of years and much revisiting of the issue (the second time). The third may be triggered by comments from others that the person has to decide how to receive: if other people think they can see in me the potential to be an ordained minister, how can I begin to discern whether or not there is any truth to their perception? And of course, the boundaries between them are not absolute either. Even in the case of Ignatius' 'first time', all kinds of questions are likely to follow about how in fact the choice is to be lived out in concrete circumstances, which may well in fact take us on to the second and third times in order to answer them.

As well as giving us a helpful map, however, the *Spiritual Exercises* suggest that if we really want to do the will of God in our vocation, we must attend closely to our own will in Christian formation. We need to listen very carefully to what we are actually willing, what we are really seeking, and not simply preach to ourselves about what ought to be the case. We also

---

101 Ignatius, 'Spiritual Exercises', p. 318.

need to be completely and resolutely focused on the purpose of our calling, and not let ourselves muddle this up with lesser goals and concerns. These two points might sound contradictory, but they are not. The purpose of our calling needs to be the clear mirror that we constantly hold up to our willing in all its complex, divided and messy reality. If we are able to do that, we make space for the work of grace in letting the love of God take ever deeper root in our hearts. As we come to recognize when our will is being moved by that love and when it is being drawn instead by the self-love of our 'old self' (Rom. 6.6), we will know well enough when we are being called on to new things and when we are called to stay where we are. And in responding to the call of God, we will find our fulfilment and all our peace.

Chapter review

In the New Testament, the love that characterizes Christians is neither an uplifting feeling nor obedience to rules, but a committed way of living that finds expression in what have traditionally been called the virtues. We need to find ways to recover this tradition if we want to be able to talk about moral formation with any confidence or precision. There will be times when our will seems deeply divided, or we experience conflicting motivations in other ways. The work of the Institute of Psychology of the Gregorian University encourages us to see opportunities here for deeper formation and provides a framework for understanding what may be happening. Finally, the treatment of election in the *Spiritual Exercises* sketches an approach for relating significant decisions, including those relating to the distinctive vocations discussed in Chapter 6, to the formation of the will through divine love.

Afterword

The call of God sends us and shapes us. It sends us out and it shapes us inwardly. Even when we say our most fervent 'Yes' to God's call, we are liable to underestimate how radical is this being sent, how radical this being shaped. It is not easy to accept that it can mean nothing less than our death and resurrection.

We do not get to choose between being sent and being shaped, between mission and formation. To see these two as in some kind of inevitable tension indicates a failure of theological thinking about vocation. To presume that our own calling can bypass one or the other discloses a flaw in our understanding of discipleship. This applies to Churches as well as to individual Christians. The purpose of our calling, as this emerged in Part 2 of the book, is becoming conformed to the image of the Son of God. This cannot happen without our being shaped in his likeness, and it cannot happen without our being sent to do his work. We cannot share the likeness without sharing the work, and we cannot enter more deeply into the work without being transformed more deeply into the likeness. For this is love's work, and we can only undertake it as the Holy Spirit begins to un-weave the chaotically enmeshed patterns of self-love in our hearts, our relationships, our communities and our institutions. Self-love is always at hand to take our best efforts at the service of others and turn them back into the reflection of ourselves.

Christian formation has always been about this unweaving of self-love's patterns through the power of the Spirit, so that 'Christ may dwell in your hearts through faith, as you are being rooted and grounded in love' (Eph. 3.17). It has always been about Christ: the central chapter of the book is the heart of the matter for us. We are not, then, the first people to be concerned with Christian formation: the language may be relatively recent, but the subject has been there from the beginning of the Church's history, and, as I hope has become apparent from Part 3 in particular, we have much to learn from the wisdom of Christian traditions over two millennia. Not the least of the ways in which our own age shows its continuity with Western modernity is in its edge of disdain for what is past and its faith that only what is made by us and for us here and now can really help us. The modern Church is certainly not exempt here.

That said, there are also some specific challenges for Christian formation today, and good reason for using this term to draw attention to them. One of the consistent issues throughout the book has been the importance of practices: we are formed as human beings by our participation in practices that communicate narratives of human fulfilment. The Church therefore needs the dedication of scholars and commentators who study the 'secular' context in which we live and can help us to discern where its dynamics are in more or less direct tension with the work of Christian formation. The three short essays in Part 1 of this book were intended to show the importance of this task and highlight some areas for reflection in relation to it. Yet while all our lives are dominated by daily participation in practices whose relation to Christian understanding is at best profoundly ambiguous, the Church itself can seem to be losing confidence in the practices that have underpinned Christian formation for much if not all of its history. Participation in public liturgy, in formal catechesis and regular theological study, in the Christian tradition of practising the virtues: each of these, taken for granted by our predecessors, may seem irreparably obsolete at the start of the twenty-first century. I have tried to argue in Part 3 that they are not. Perhaps I am wrong. But if I am, Christian formation, and therefore Christian mission, can only be sustained by finding new practices that enable the gospel's paradoxical narrative of death and resurrection to become embedded in the fabric of our lives. Following from Chapter 6, I would also add that such practices need to flow from the sacrament of baptism and into the sacrament of the Eucharist as primary, church-constituting practices.

I imagine that few people reading this book will need persuading that Christian formation really matters. Yet most of us, at some point or another, struggle to make the space for it – to take the time for it. Formation takes time. Is there an internal sigh when we hear that? Modernity encourages us to see time as a limited commodity for our use, to be ready to protect 'our' time from those things that might 'take' it from us, and to find satisfaction in accounting for the use of our time in terms of productive output. Christian doctrine, however, teaches us that time is an integral part of the goodness of God's creation: it is space for our growth into the fullness of God's purposes, as I tried to show in Chapter 4. God's gift to us in Jesus Christ comes to us as creatures: temporal, embodied creatures. To receive this gift takes us time; it fills our time with grace. Our shaping, like our sending, must work with the various overlapping rhythms of human life in time: biological, psychological, cultural, social. Neither formation nor mission can aspire to short-circuit all of that and work through a parallel dimension. This is not a difficult sentence, to be met with brave resignation suppressing our resentment. It is matter for infinite joy that the eternal God draws near to us in time and takes our time into eternal life.

Further Reading

Aspects of Christian formation

Dietrich Bonhoeffer, 1954, *Life Together*, ET, London: SCM.

Ellen T. Charry, 1997, *By the Renewing of Your Minds: The Pastoral Function of Christian Doctrine*, Oxford: Oxford University Press.

Charles R. Foster, Lisa Dahill, Lawrence A. Golemon and Barbara Wang Tolentino, 2006, *Educating Clergy: Teaching Practices and Pastoral Imagination*, San Francisco: Jossey-Bass.

Denham Grierson, 1984, *Transforming a People of God*, Melbourne: The Joint Board of Christian Education of Australia and New Zealand.

Robert Davis Hughes III, 2008, *Beloved Dust: Tides of the Spirit in the Christian Life*, New York: Continuum.

Franco Imoda (ed.), 2000, *A Journey to Freedom: An Interdisciplinary Approach to the Anthropology of Formation*, Studies in Spirituality Supplement 5, Leuven: Peeters.

Christopher Irvine, 2005, *The Art of God: The Making of Christians and the Meaning of Worship*, London: SPCK.

Alasdair MacIntyre, 2009, *Dependent Rational Animals: Why Human Beings Need the Virtues*, rev. edn, London: Duckworth.

Martyn Percy, 2010, *Shaping the Church: The Promise of Implicit Theology*, Farnham: Ashgate.

Simon Tugwell, 1985, *Ways of Imperfection: An Exploration of Christian Spirituality*, Springfield, Illinois: Templegate.

Samuel Wells, 2006, *God's Companions: Reimagining Christian Ethics*, Malden, Massachusetts: Blackwell.

Tom Wright, 2010, *Virtue Reborn*, London: SPCK.

Understanding the human person

Marc Cortez, 2010, *Theological Anthropology: A Guide for the Perplexed*, London: T. & T. Clark.

Doctrine Commission of the General Synod of the Church of England, 2003, *Being Human: A Christian Understanding of Personhood Illustrated with Reference to Power, Money, Sex and Time*, London: Church House Publishing.

Stanley J. Grenz, 2001, *The Social God and the Relational Self: A Trinitarian Theology of the* Imago Dei, Louisville, Kentucky: Westminster John Knox.

L. M. Rulla, 1986, *Anthropology of the Christian Vocation*, Vol. 1, *Interdisciplinary Bases*, Rome: Gregorian University Press.

Christoph Schwöbel and Colin E. Gunton (eds), 1991, *Persons, Divine and Human: King's College Essays in Theological Anthropology*, Edinburgh: T. & T. Clark.

R. Kendall Soulen and Linda Woodhead (eds), 2006, *God and Human Dignity*, Grand Rapids, Michigan: Eerdmans.

Kevin Vanhoozer, 1997, 'Human Being, Individual and Social', in Colin E. Gunton (ed.), *The Cambridge Companion to Christian Doctrine*, Cambridge: Cambridge University Press, pp. 158–88.

World Council of Churches, 2005, *Christian Perspectives on Theological Anthropology: A Faith and Order Study Document*, Faith and Order Paper 199, Geneva: WCC.

John D. Zizioulas, 1997, *Being as Communion: Studies in Personhood and the Church*, Crestwood, New York: St Vladimir's Seminary Press.

John D. Zizioulas, 2006, *Communion and Otherness: Further Studies in Personhood and the Church*, ed. Paul McPartlan, London: T. & T. Clark.

Index

Abraham 109, 129
Adam 47–8, 52, 54, 140
Adam and Eve 49, 66, 73
anamnesis 113–14, 121
Aquinas, Thomas 142–3,
    152
Aristotle 3
Augustine 51, 102, 119,
    143, 152, 159–60

baptism xiii, 41, 66, 68,
    80–3, 85–6, 93, 95,
    98–101, 105, 133, 135,
    155, 171
Barth, Karl 48, 74, 130n
body of Christ 81, 85, 92,
    101, 153, 156
Bonhoeffer, Dietrich 112n,
    116

calling xiii–iv, 40–1, 47, 49,
    50–1, 55, 58–9, 69, 75–
    7, 89, 98, 105–6, 109,
    115, 119–20, 163, 169

purpose of our 41, 79,
    82, 90, 97, 100, 141,
    148, 153, 166–9
catechesis 133, 170
Charry, Ellen T. 74n, 137n
childhood 5, 8, 23, 28–9,
    118–19
Christology 40, 64
command 45, 47, 51–2, 54,
    58, 67, 110–11, 122,
    150–51
commandment 37, 58, 110–
    11, 149–51
communion xiii, 41, 71–2,
    76, 78–9, 84, 89, 99,
    101–2, 120–21, 1234,
    142–5, 166
congregation ix, 25, 96, 103,
    114, 117, 132, 146, 163
creation xiv, 14, 40–1, 43–
    8, 50–6, 58, 60, 62, 67,
    73–6, 78, 85, 88–9, 99,
    109, 113–14, 122, 127,
    141, 143–5, 166, 171

cross 62, 64, 74, 82, 90, 122
crucified 82, 84, 113, 144,
    150, 156
culture xiv, 1, 3–4, 6–7, 9,
    13–15, 18, 29, 33, 35–6,
    46, 55, 75, 81, 94, 96,
    102–3, 109, 115, 119,
    128, 132, 134, 156

desire 5–6, 14, 21, 23, 29–
    30, 35, 67, 79, 81, 90,
    102, 117, 124, 146,
    154, 156, 159–61
  for God 123, 142–3, 150,
    160
discipleship xii–xiii, 5, 36, 40,
    63, 75, 79–80, 100–1,
    112, 136, 141, 166, 169
duty 11, 33, 36, 38, 113,
    156, 160, 163

Easter 112–13
egoism 34–7, 94, 127–30,
    146
Enlightenment 8–9, 19–20,
    22–3, 25–6
Eucharist 41, 80–6, 88,
    91–2, 97–8, 105, 112,
    156, 171

faith x, 10, 25–6, 52–3, 56,
    58–9, 62, 65–6, 68–9,
    75–6, 78, 82–3, 89, 92,

97, 105, 110, 114, 118,
    129–31, 133–4, 136,
    152, 159–60, 170
faithfulness 37, 80, 101
  of Jesus 69, 76
  of God 63, 67, 88, 90,
    109–10, 120–21, 124
formation, ministerial xiin,
    xiv, 92–3, 96, 101,
    153, 167
freedom 4–11, 13–15, 17, 19,
    21–3, 26–9, 31–4, 36–8,
    50, 52, 54–5, 68, 80, 94,
    102, 121, 148–9
  of God 43, 91, 120
Freud, Sigmund 12n, 21–3,
    118, 161

Genesis 43–8, 50, 53–4, 56,
    73, 87
gift 27, 45, 52, 55–6, 66–7,
    74, 111, 115, 120–21,
    125, 135, 141, 144–5,
    148, 160, 171
  of language 48, 126
gifts 79, 84, 91–2, 102, 140,
    143, 150
grace 41, 59, 64, 75, 83, 89,
    113, 119, 142, 144,
    150, 157–9, 163, 168,
    171
Gregory of Nyssa 146
Gregory the Great 157

Grenz, Stanley 45n, 73n
Guigo II 123, 145

Hadewijch 152–3
Holy Spirit 71–2, 91, 95–6,
    101–3, 105, 119, 123,
    125, 150–1, 160, 169
Hooker, Richard 144
Horkheimer, Max 128n
household 87–90, 96
humanity 10, 14, 20, 22, 40–
    1, 43–8, 50–2, 54–6,
    58–9, 65, 68, 72–4, 76,
    79, 81, 83, 109, 141,
    145–6, 150, 159–60

identity 3, 6, 11, 13–14, 17,
    26, 33, 63, 70, 91, 124
Ignatius Loyola 124, 164–7
image xii, 41, 44–6, 48–9,
    51, 55–6, 59, 71–3,
    75–9, 82, 85, 88–9,
    97–9, 102, 146, 148–
    50, 166, 169
incarnation xiv, 59, 63,
    73–5
individualism 34
    expressive 11, 14–15, 21,
    37, 106, 109, 156
Institute of Psychology,
    Gregorian University
    x, 161–2, 168
Irenaeus 54

Irvine, Christopher 113n,
    114n
Israel 58–60, 62, 65, 69, 83,
    109–11, 121, 149–50

Kavanagh, Aidan xiiin, 131n
knowledge 4, 10, 17–24,
    26–9, 31–2, 35, 38,
    50–2, 54–5, 64, 66, 80,
    102, 115, 119, 121,
    127–8, 132, 135, 137,
    139–41, 165

Jesus xii, 17, 20, 41, 59–76,
    78–9, 82–4, 89, 97,
    102, 105, 115, 120,
    122–3, 149–51, 171
Job 129–30
John 17, 28, 59, 62–3, 66–
    72, 105, 126

Kant 19

law 7, 33, 36, 82, 111, 149,
    159
Lewis, C. S. 24
liturgy 85, 113n, 114–16,
    118, 121–2, 125, 131,
    170
Lonergan, Bernard 138–9,
    141
love 4, 10, 28–38, 49–50, 52–
    5, 64, 70–2, 77, 80, 102,

113, 120–1, 127, 130, 143, 145–6, 149–53, 156–61, 164, 168–70
Lubac, Henri de 43n, 143

MacIntyre, Alasdair 22n, 25n, 154
Macquarrie, John 54n
marriage xii, 31, 37, 50, 89–90, 94–7, 164
Maximus the Confessor 74
memory 84, 102, 105–8, 111–12, 117–20, 122, 124–5
Merton, Thomas 145n
Middle Ages 8, 73, 122, 137
ministry ix–xiv, 14, 36, 40–1, 56, 75, 91–7, 100, 103, 135, 162–4, 167
of Jesus 60, 62, 65, 68
orders of 93–4, 96
of the Spirit 126
mission xiii–xiv, 60, 81, 169, 171
modernity xiv, 8–10, 12, 24, 27, 31–2, 114, 137, 148–9, 170–1
Moses 109–11

narrative 1, 19, 45, 50, 63, 81, 108, 117, 129, 171
'grand narratives' 9, 12
of human fulfilment 4, 7–8, 10, 80–1, 83, 97, 170

Paul 2, 5–6, 12, 48, 78, 82–3, 89, 91, 150–2, 154, 156, 159, 165
person, human 39, 48–50, 53, 57, 75, 79, 97, 121, 126, 142–3, 146
person, divine 70
personhood 15, 23, 50, 63, 72, 76, 83, 120–1, 125
Plato 18–19, 30, 119
postmodern 9
promises, God's 41, 59, 60, 62, 105
prayer 51, 69, 84–5, 88, 90–1, 100, 102, 112–14, 121–3, 131–2, 135, 143, 145, 158, 163
psychology 7, 21–3, 117, 125
cognitive 108
depth 118–19, 121, 160

responsibility 15, 26, 36, 38, 46–7, 49, 55, 68, 87, 90, 93–4, 96, 100–1, 116, 155, 157, 164
resurrection 76, 81–3, 97, 119–20, 145, 156, 169, 171
Richard of St Victor 71
ritual 108–10
Rosenzweig, Franz 150n
Rulla, L. M. 40n, 161n, 162n

salvation xiv, 74–5, 146, 150, 166
scepticism 21, 138–9
Scotus, John Duns 74
Scripture 25, 50, 73, 83–5, 90–2, 112, 116, 121–2, 125, 131, 144–5, 150
selfhood 49, 79, 83, 106, 108–9, 117–19, 160
seminary ix, 103, 136, 146, 162
service 33, 35–6, 80, 84, 100, 112, 131–2, 148, 150, 166, 169
sin 2–3, 44, 53, 55–8, 62–4, 66–7, 74–5, 78–9, 84, 88, 94, 113, 119–21, 124–5, 143, 148, 159, 163
Spaemann, Robert 72n
Spinoza 8, 26
spirituality 14, 36, 40, 103, 119, 144

Taylor, Charles 3n, 11, 14–15, 114n
therapy 23, 119, 125
tradition, Christian xiv, 25, 120, 122, 124, 145, 152, 163, 170

Trinity 41, 71, 78, 102

unconscious 23, 118–20, 160, 162

Vatican II 48
Vanhoozer, Kevin 23n, 43n
virtue 151–8, 168, 170
vocations, distinctive xii, 41, 86–7, 89–90, 93, 95–7, 100–1, 164, 168

Wells, Sam 86n, 153n
wisdom 30, 34, 55, 65, 75, 95, 127–30, 136–8, 140, 163, 170
witness xiii, 79, 83–4, 87, 100, 112, 131–2, 153
work 1, 6, 12, 18, 33, 41, 47, 49, 55, 62, 87–90, 92, 94–5, 97, 100, 106, 110
worship xi, 36–7, 58, 68, 80, 83–4, 91, 112–16, 122, 125, 132, 135, 157–8, 160
Wright, N. T./Tom 62n, 152n

Zizioulas, John 51n, 72n